Forensic Science

**Laboratory Experiment
Manual and Workbook**

Forensic Science

Laboratory Experiment Manual and Workbook

Thomas Kubic
Nicholas Petraco

CRC PRESS

Boca Raton   London   New York   Washington, D.C.

Library of Congress Cataloging-in-Publication Data

Kubic, Thomas.
    Forensic science laboratory experiment manual and workbook / Thomas Kubic, Nicholas Petraco.
        p.   cm.
    ISBN 0-8493-1508-5 (alk. paper)
        1. Forensic sciences—Handbooks, manuals, etc. 2. Criminal investigation—Handbooks,
    manuals, etc. 3. Evidence, Criminal—Handbooks, manuals, etc. 4. Crime
    laboratories—Handbooks, manuals, etc.   I. Petraco, Nicholas. II. Title.

    HV8073 .K75 2002
    363.25—dc21   2002031323
                                                                                              CIP

Visit the CRC Press Web site at www.crcpress.com

No claim to original U.S. Government works
International Standard Book Number 0-8493-1508-5
Library of Congress Card Number 2002031323
Printed in the United States of America   3 4 5 6 7 8 9 0
Printed on acid-free paper

Preface

Forensic Science Laboratory Experiment Manual and Workbook satisfies a need for basic forensic experiments. This manual is appropriate for laboratory classes beginning from high school level on. Most of the experiments require equipment that is readily available in any science laboratory. They are uniformly inexpensive and safe to perform.

This manual is intended to be used in conjunction with any current forensic textbook, but most especially with:

Forensic Science: An Introduction to Scientific and Investigative Techniques, edited by Stuart James and Jon Nordby, CRC Press LLC, Boca Raton, FL, 2003.

Criminalistics: An Introduction to Forensic Science, 7th ed., by Richard Saferstein, Prentice-Hall, Upper Saddle River, NJ, 2001.

The authors appreciate all suggestions for improving future editions of this manual and may be contacted at taka.micro@verizon.net and nlp101648@aol.com.

List of Equipment and Supplies

This inventory lists the materials needed for the forensic laboratory experiments outlined in this laboratory workbook. Each item listed should be made available for sharing by groups of two or three students unless otherwise noted.

General Laboratory Equipment

- Bright field compound microscopes with 4×, 10×, 20×, and 40× achromatic objective lenses, 10× oculars (eyepieces), and in-base illumination systems with focusable condensers
- Two polarizing microscopes, one with a trinocular head
- Stereomicroscopes with magnification ranges of 4× to 40×
- Eyepieces with reticle scales for stereomicroscopes and compound microscopes or have reticles installed in existing units
- Stage micrometers for reflected light or high quality scale in mm
- Stage micrometers for compound microscope, 1 mm in 1/100 division
- Hand-held magnifying glasses, 5× to 10×, or linen testers
- One half gross of 25 mm by 75 mm precleaned glass microscope slides
- Assortment of No. 1 ½ glass cover glasses: square (18 mm), rectangular (22 mm × 40 mm and 22 mm × 50 mm), round (18 mm)
- Plastic microscope slides
- Assortment of mounting media: distilled water, Permount, Cargille Melt Mount® 1.539, Cargille refractive index oil set A
- Plastic rulers (metric and English scales)
- Protractors
- Tape measures, metric/U.S., 1 to 50 feet
- Two fine, nonmagnetic, stainless steel tweezers
- Trace evidence vacuum with 25 traps
- Two rolls of dust lifting tape
- Two stainless steel dissecting needles with holders
- No. 11 scalpel
- Microspatula
- Box of flat, wooden toothpicks

- Small scissors with pointed tip
- Equipment for thin layer chromatography: 25 mm × 75 mm, silica gel plates, reagents (sprays, solvents), glassware, tanks with covers, 12 Coplin jars with covers, blotter paper, microspotting pipettes
- Ultraviolet light with short and long wavelengths
- Platinum loop with holder
- Small magnets
- pH paper, 0 to 14
- Thermometer, 0 to 100°C
- Alcohol lamp
- Balances, readability 1 mg to 1000 gm
- Assorted micro- and macro-disposable pipettes
- Aluminum weighing dishes, 60 mm diameter (100 per semester)
- Graduated glass cylinders, 1 to 50 ml (0.5 or 1.0 ml subdivisions)
- Disposable petri dishes, 75 to 125 mm
- Cellophane tape
- Three 35mm Minolta or Nikon cameras with detachable flashes and lenses
- Photographic scales
- Tripods
- Black-and-white film
- Color film (to be processed commercially)
- Miscellaneous camera accessories
- Darkroom (with electricity and water) and equipment for black-and-white film development and printing, including an enlarger, photographic paper, chemicals, and other required equipment

Fingerprint Supplies

- 12 fingerprint feather dusters
- 12 fiberglass latent brushes
- Four magnetic applicator brushes
- Assortment of white, black, magnet, and fluorescent dusting powders
- 12 rolls of 2 in. lifting tape with dispensers
- Four black and four white gloss card pads, 50 cards per pad, 3 in. × 5 in. and 8 1/2 in. × 11 in.
- 100 2 in. × 2 in. white hinged lifters
- Super Glue for fuming
- Warming plates
- Glue dishes
- Five fingerprint ink pads
- 250 fingerprint cards

- Two fingerprint stands with pads and rollers
- Alternative forensic light source
- Ultraviolet light source

Footprint Processing Equipment

- Electrostatic dust print lifter
- 25 lb box of dental casting materials
- Six 1-pint plastic bottles for distilled water
- 250 clear footwear lifting sheets with covers
- Old footwear

Tool Mark Supplies

- Assorted hand tools: wire cutters, cable cutters, saws, drills, screw drivers, leather-man tool, etc.
- Assorted locks
- Pieces of wood and metal
- Pieces of aluminum rods and plates
- Silicone casting

Evidence Packing Equipment

- Evidence envelopes
- Evidence boxes
- Evidence bags
- Evidence containers
- Evidence tape

General Forensic Laboratory Safety Rules

- Wear approved safety eyeglasses at all times to protect against splashes of chemicals, explosions, and blunt impacts. Normal eyeglasses do not meet these requirements.
- Wear protective clothing in the laboratory.
- Notify the instructor immediately of an accident, fire, or dangerous condition.
- Learn the locations of and how to operate all laboratory safety equipment: eye wash, safety shower, fire hose, fire extinguisher, fire blanket, and neutralizing chemical agents such as potash.
- If a chemical splashes into your eyes, immediately wash your eyes with cold water for at least 30 minutes. Use freely flowing cold water from the eye wash or sink.
- Immediately extinguish all fires. Remove all affected clothing under the safety shower. Use wet towels or fire blankets to suffocate the fire.
- Immediately neutralize all chemical spills with neutralizing agents to be found in the hood, in spill buckets, or designated areas.
- Always work with chemicals under ventilation hoods to avoid the inhalation of potentially harmful fumes.
- Secure, tie up, or cover long hair to prevent accidental burning or getting hair caught in equipment.
- Wash all laboratory glassware before use. Never add chemicals to soiled glassware.
- Keep the laboratory and your working area clean and free from clutter.
- Do not eat, drink, or smoke in the laboratory.
- Prevent biological hazards. Wear a protective laboratory coat, apron, or other outer clothing and remove it immediately after leaving the laboratory.
- Wash your hands thoroughly after handling anything in the laboratory.
- Never perform an unauthorized experiment or procedure.
- Do not deviate from the instructions of your professor or your laboratory manual. Never perform a laboratory procedure or experiment you are uncertain about. Ask your instructor for clarification.
- Never pipette by mouth. Always use a suction bulb.
- Do not force glass tubing into a rubber stopper. Lubricate the tubing and protect your hands with gloves.
- Never work alone in the laboratory.
- Immediately seek medical attention for cuts, burns, and other serious injuries.
- Follow other safety rules established by your instructor.

Scientific Measurements and Errors: Determination of Density of Glass

Purposes

This experiment has three purposes:

1. Making a number of measurements, including length, weight, and liquid volume determinations.
2. Determining variations of measurements of the same items by multiple students.
3. Optional exercises include determining standard deviations (variabilities) of measurements, and determining density of glass by measurement of mass and volume of shards.

Equipment and Supplies

1. Plastic scale or ruler with numbered inch and millimeter scales.
2. Plastic protractor calibrated in 1-degree increments as a minimum. Increments should be numbered.
3. Electronic or triple beam balance with readability to at least 0.01 g; readability to 1 mg would be better.
4. Glass transfer pipettes to deliver 10 mL.
5. Disposable aluminum (60 mm × 15 mm) or plastic weighing dishes able to contain 20 to 40 mL of liquid.
6. Glass graduated cylinders of 25- or 50-mL capacity graduated in 1-mL increments; graduations of 0.5 mL would be better.
7. Deionized or distilled water.
8. Assorted beakers: 100 mL, 25 mL, etc.
9. Glass shards from sides and bottom of a broken bottle; shards should be 1 cm × 1 cm in size.

10. Tape measures: 12-ft divided into numbered 1/16 in. increments; 25- or 50-ft divided into numbered 1/8 in. increments.

Procedure

Part I: Measurements

Employing a scale and protractor, measure the sides of the structure shown in Figure 1.1 to the nearest 0.5 mm. Measure angles A and B to the nearest 0.5 degree. Record the data and the identifying number or letters of your scale and protractor below. (Your instructor may instruct you to record the data on a blackboard or on the class data sheet on page 7.)

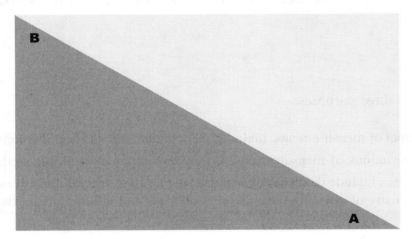

FIGURE 1.1

Calculate the average of two of your classmates' measurements recorded on the blackboard or data sheet using the following equation:

$$\bar{x} = \Sigma\, x_i\, /\, n$$

where $\bar{x}$ = average, x_i = total sum of all data points, and n = number of data points.

Employing the 12-ft tape, measure an object designated by your instructor (e.g., a desk or blackboard) to the nearest 1/16 in. and record the dimensions below. Employing a longer tape, measure a larger area designated by the instructor. Record the dimensions. Calculate the average of the measurements made by all students in your class.

Optional Exercise: Variability and Standard Deviation

Determine the variability of these measurements by calculating the standard deviation of each measurement by using the following equation:

$$S = [\Sigma\, (x - x_i)^2_j\, /\, n - 1]^{1/2}$$

Your instructor will explain how to perform the calculation manually and the meaning of standard deviation. Other equations that calculate standard deviation are valid and may be used. You may use a scientific calculator.

Part II: Weighing and Volume Calculations

Obtain an item or items from the instructor and weigh it or them to the nearest division readable on your balance. Record the weights and note brief descriptions of the items and their weights on the data sheet. Calculate the class average weight for each item.

Obtain a weighing boat and weigh it. Pipette two or three 10-mL measurements of water into the boat. Reweigh the boat. Determine the weight of the water by subtracting the weight of the boat. Record your data below.

Assuming water has a density of 1 g/mL, calculate the volume of water transferred.

$$\text{Density } (\rho) = (\text{mass in g/volume in mL}) \qquad (1.1)$$

Calculate percent error.

$$\text{Percent error} = \text{mL of transferred water} - \text{volume from pipetted water/mL of transferred water} \times 100 \qquad (1.2)$$

Calculate the average mL transferred by each 10 mL pipette operation. Record the percent error and average mL below.

Optional Exercise: Calculating Density of Glass

Obtain, clean, and dry a few pieces of broken bottle glass. Obtain a graduated cylinder (Figure 1.2 shows a 25-mL cylinder with an English/metric ruler) and fill to approximately half its volume with water. Record the volume to the nearest 0.1 mL. Weigh one or more pieces of glass totaling 3 to 6 g to the highest readability. Carefully place (do not splash) the glass pieces into the graduate. Record the new volume. Determine the volume change ($V_{end} - V_{start}$), which is the volume of the glass (V_{glass}). Read the meniscus (Figure 1.2). Record your data below.

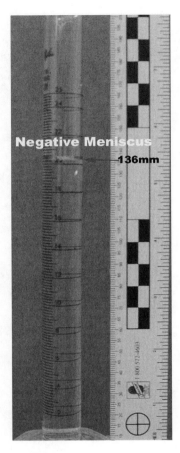

FIGURE 1.2

Calculate the density of the glass:

$$\rho = mg/VmL$$

Data Form

Use the data form on the next page to record the figures from your work and your classmates' work as per your instructor's directions. Transfer the appropriate data to the report section that follows the data sheet.

EXPERIMENT 1 DATA SHEET

NAME_____   DATE_____

Enter measurements in the proper spaces. Note equipment identification in parentheses (e.g., for Side 1: 22.5 mm (B)). Enter measurement/weight data on the lines next to your student number. Enter your classmates' data on the lines next to their numbers.

Student #	Side 1	Side 2	A	B	Desk	Floor	Weights A	Weights B	Weights C	Eq. 1.3*	Eq. 1.4**
1											
2											
3											
4											
5											
6											
7											
8											
9											
10											
11											
12											

* Equation 1.3
    Weight in grams of pipetted water/No. of mL of pipetted water.
** Equation 1.4
    Density of glass = mass in grams/volume in mL.

Report

Document the following in your report:

1. Length and angle measurements

2. Class averages and standard deviations

3. Weight determinations

4. Average volume of water transferred

5. Percent error

6. Density of glass

7. Class averages for weights of objects A through C

8. Percent error for water weight, transfer experiment

9. Short narrative of what you learned from these exercises

2

Understanding Elements of Identification and Individualization

Purposes

Acquaint the student with the concepts of identification and individualization employed in forensic science. Each student will learn to distinguish class characteristics, wear characteristics, and individualizing characteristics. Everyone involved in recognition, documentation, collection, examination, identification, and evaluation of physical evidence should clearly understand the distinctions.

Class characteristics are features shared by all members of a certain class or group of animals, plants, or other objects. For example, all human beings are biologically classified as *Homo sapiens* even though they look very different. All humans have two arms, two legs, one trunk, one head, and other features that classify them as human. Other characteristics of humans can be used to further classify them as males or females.

The features that classify groups are known as class characteristics. While class characteristics can be used to categorize individuals, they are not unique enough to individualize or associate items of physical evidence to a common origin.

If a piece of an item of clothing was missing and a piece of the same fabric matching the size and shape of the missing piece from the damaged garment was found in a suspect's vehicle, one could state conclusively that the questionable piece of fabric originated from the damaged article of clothing. This is an example of individualization — the pattern of class characteristics and unique individualizing characteristics of the item of clothing and the piece of fabric were found to fit together in a physical match, such as a jigsaw match.

In this exercise, we will use photographs of a shoe sole to discuss the basic concepts of identification and individualization. Students will then have an opportunity to identify, characterize, and individualize other objects.

Equipment and Supplies

1. Photographs of a shoe sole
2. Ruler
3. Protractor
3. Assorted old and new tools, two red apples, two pairs of blue jeans, two chairs, two monogrammed cups, and two silk-screened T-shirts
4. Two of the same types of items (for example, No. 2 pencils) provided by the student
5. Two items provided by the instructor

Procedure

1. Review Figures 2.1 and 2.2 and/or study the photographs provided by your instructor. What is similar about them? How do they differ?

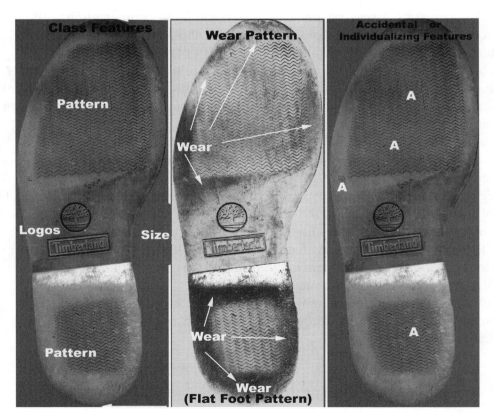

FIGURE 2.1

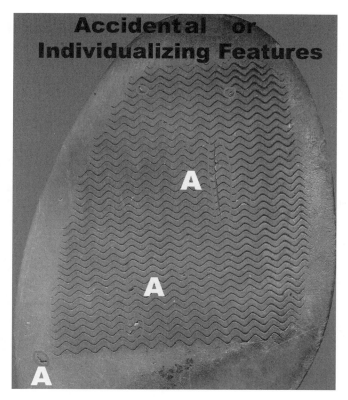

FIGURE 2.2

2. Describe the class characteristics attributed to these items by their manufacturer.

3. Describe the characteristics caused by their use or wear.

4. Describe the characteristics that are attributable to an individual item.

5. Examine the two items provided by the instructor. Discuss their class features, wear features, and individualizing features.

Report

1. Can you individualize or describe each item? How would you do so?

2. Define class characteristics.

3. Define wear pattern.

4. Define accidental characteristic.

5. Define identity.

6. Define classification.

7. Define individualization.

8. Write a report discussing your findings after examining two items provided by your instructor.

Use of the Compound Microscope

Purposes

A compound light microscope is one of the most valuable instruments in a crime laboratory. A basic transmitted light microscope may be complemented by a stereomicroscope, polarized light microscope (PLM), phase contrast microscope (PCM), and visible and infrared microspectrophotometers. These instruments can be used for sample preparation, preliminary examinations, or as final analytical tools.

These instruments are called *compound microscopes* because the final magnification or apparent size of the image is computed by multiplying the objective (primary or first lens) power by the eyepiece (ocular) power. For example, a common combination is a 10× objective employed with a 10× eyepiece for a total magnification of 100× (10× primary power multiplied by 10× ocular power = 100× magnification).

The quality of the image depends on the quality of the lenses and proper alignment of the microscope. The lenses vary from inexpensive (uncorrected) to moderate (simply corrected or achromatic) to the very expensive (highly corrected or apochromatic). The following terms describe certain important concepts of microscopy.

Working distance — Distance from the top of the specimen (when in focus) to the lower tip of the objective; as a general rule, the greater the magnification, the shorter the working distance.

Depth of focus — Thickness of parts of the sample that appear to be in acceptable focus (clear and sharp) simultaneously. The greater the magnification, the smaller the depth of field.

Field of view — Size (area or diameter of visible field) of the specimen that can be viewed.

Numerical aperture (NA) — Equation describing the relationship of the angle (AA) of light that the objective collects and the refractive index (n) of the medium between the specimen and the objective. It is important to the determination of resolving power. $NA = n \times \sin AA/2$. The NA varies with magnification for similar quality objectives.

Resolving power (RP) — The smallest details separated by a distance equal in size to the details that can be determined to be separate objects. RP relates to the NA, the wavelength (λ) of the light employed, and a constant (k) equal to 0.61, and sensitivity of the human eye. $RP = 0.61 \times \lambda/NA$. The smaller the RP, the smaller the observable detail.

Refractive index (n) — Ratio of the speed of light in a vacuum divided by the speed in the medium of interest. For visible light, the index is always equal to or greater than 1.

In this experiment, you will practice the procedure for proper alignment of a light microscope and observe selected materials at various magnifications.

Equipment and Supplies

1. Transmitted light compound microscope with illuminator
2. Microscope slides and cover slips
3. Sample manipulation tools: dissection needles, index cards, weighing paper, weighing boats, small scissors, tweezers, scalpels, cellophane tape, small plastic or glass vials with caps or corks, unsharpened pencils with erasers
4. Tissues and lens paper
5. Oil of cloves (n = 1.543), oil of cedar (n = 1.505), α-monobromonaphthalene (n = 1.66) or commercial oils having similar n values
6. Set of mounted forensic reference materials
7. Human hair, tea, tobacco, synthetic fibers, cotton fibers

Procedure

1. Review your notes on microscope alignment.
2. Review Figure 3.1 to become familiar with the microscope and its parts.
3. Align the microscope as described in your notes or the alignment instructions below. Take note of any minor differences your instructor points out in your microscope or the procedure to be followed.
4. Starting at a low magnification (about 40×) and increase it (about 100×), align the microscope based on your instructor's instructions. Record your observations and, on a separate sheet, make clear drawings of what you see.

5. Carefully observe the instructor's demonstration of the method of mounting a sample in an immersion medium (liquid, gas, or solid surrounding a sample). Employing 100× magnification, mount and observe loose samples that the instructor selects in at least two different mounting liquids. Record any differences you observe.

Alignment Instructions

Proper microscope alignment is essential to obtaining high quality images and ensuring that the instrument performs up to its capability. Köhler illumination is a method of aligning the microscope so that the optical components are in the correct positions, distortion is minimized, illumination is bright and uniform and concentrates on the area around the sample of interest, and extraneous glare and light are eliminated.

   The components that may need adjustment are the (1) light source, (2) field diaphragm, (3) focus, (4) condenser focus, and (5) condenser diaphragm. The terms *iris* and *aperture* are often interchanged with *diaphragm*. Certain microscope manufacturers adjust certain parameters in the factory to ensure certain performance levels, so not all five components can always be adjustable. The microscope user may have to adjust the interpupillary distance on the binocular viewing head and the eyepiece focus to account for differences in diopter and allow comfortable and strainless viewing. Figure 3.1 shows microscope components. Figure 3.2 illustrates appearance of the fields of view for establishing Köhler illumination.

1. Place the objective you intend to employ (usually 10×) into position. Turn on the illumination (if adjustable, ask your instructor about the voltage setting). Place a specimen on the stage.

2. Using the course focus, carefully bring the objective 1 to 2 mm above the sample by checking the space from the side of the microscope. View the specimen through the eyepieces and carefully adjust the course focus up (to increase the working distance) until the sample is in focus. The focus need not be perfect.

3. Adjust the interpupillary distance so that the field of view is round and you see a single image. At least one eyepiece usually has a focus adjustment. Close the eye that uses the eyepiece with the adjustment and critically focus the sample with the fine focus. Open that eye and close your other eye. Critically focus the image using **only** the adjustment for the eyepiece on the microscope head. The upper portion of the microscope is now properly adjusted. (See Figure 3.2)

4. Close the field iris so that it can be seen in the field of view or specimen plane. Do NOT change the focus. Center the image of the iris around the center of the specimen in the center of the field of view. Focus the image of the iris by raising and lowering the condenser using its focus

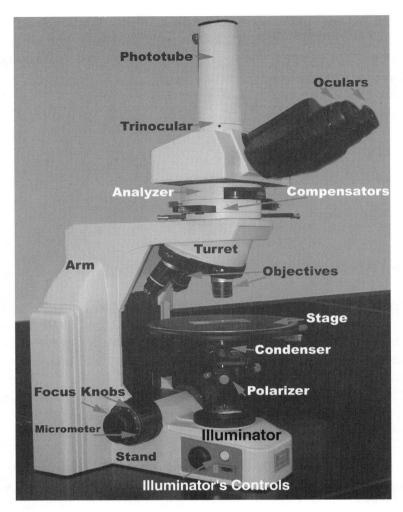

FIGURE 3.1

control. Some student microscopes do not allow these adjustments. Open the field iris until it is just outside the field of view.

5. The best designs allow the illuminator filament to be seen in the back focal plane or the objective. No frosted glass diffuser should obstruct the light path. Many modern laboratory microscopes have precentered and focused bulbs and diffusers that cannot be removed. If this is the case, you cannot go any farther with this part of the alignment procedure. Read the following paragraph and then skip to Step 6. Ask your instructor for guidance.

The back focal plane can be viewed in any of three ways. The user can remove the eyepiece and look down the microscope tube. The back focal plane can be seen. By opening and closing the condenser aperture, the user can see the image of the iris. An enlarged, more easily seen image of the focal plane is possible if a special eyepiece called a *phase telescope* or *centering telescope* replaces the normal eyepiece. The observer can also use a special auxiliary lens (called a *Bertrand lens*) built into the microscope as an option for viewing the enlarged image.

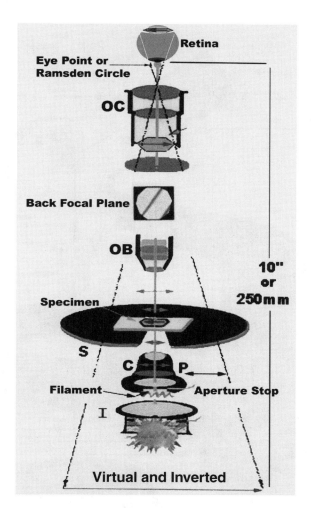

FIGURE 3.2

Turn down the intensity of the filament so that it is dull red and not bright enough to cause discomfort. While viewing the back focal plane, use the bulb centering and focusing controls to center, focus the filament, and fill the focal plane with the image of the filament.

Close the condenser iris until 70 to 80% of the diameter of the focal plane view remains unblocked.

6. Restore the optical configuration so that the specimen can be viewed properly through both eyepieces. During viewing, always make critical adjustments with the fine focus.

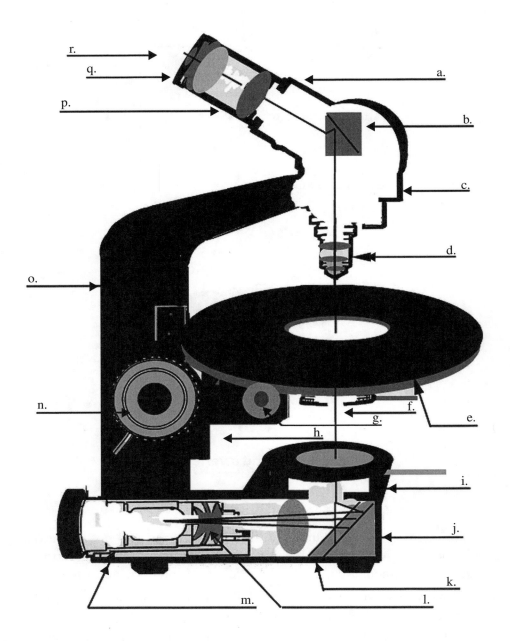

FIGURE 3.3

Report

1. Label the parts of the microscope depicted in Figure 3.3.

a. _____   j. _____

b. _____   k. _____

c. _____   l. _____

d. _____   m. _____

e. _____   n. _____

f. _____   o. _____

g. _____   p. _____

h. _____   q. _____

i. _____   r. _____

2. Use the space below to write a report of your observations; support your observations with the drawings you made (see Procedure, Step 4).

3. Write a short narrative explaining what you learned by doing this exercise.

4

Stereomicroscopes and Firing Pin Impressions (Tool Marks)

Purpose

This experiment has two stages. In the first, the student will learn about the value of the stereobinocular (dissecting) microscope, a device often used to search for trace evidence on the clothing of a suspect or victim, and view items that may have picked up transfer evidence. Stereomicroscopes are used regularly for preliminary examinations of many classes of evidence such as paint, powdered drugs, marijuana, and fibers. They are also useful for preparing samples for further analysis with other techniques such as x-ray diffraction, microspectrophotometry, and scanning electron microscopy.

The stereomicroscope can assist in measuring items of trace evidence if it is equipped with an eyepiece that includes a reticle that has a measurement scale. The scale must be calibrated so that the user knows the projected dimension of each division of the eyepiece scale at each magnification to be used for measurements. In this exercise, the student will calibrate the eyepiece scale with a standard, use the scale to perform a number of measurements, and observe the surface characteristics of some common items.

The second part of this experiment involves the comparison of a number of cartridge case, firing pin impressions in an attempt to establish common origin.

Equipment and Supplies

1. Stereomicroscope (zoom preferred) approximately 5 to 40× or 10 and 20× dual magnification with reflected light illuminator; eyepiece equipped with an ocular scale is a preferred option
2. Reflected light stage scale or millimeter scale to be used for ocular scale calibration (Figure 4.1)
3. Light blue or light green 3 × 5 index cards, glass or disposable petri dishes 75 to 125 mm in diameter, scalpel, at least two dissection needles, microspatula, small scissors, tweezers

4. Selected items for examination such as typewritten material, photocopied material, color printing from a magazine, paper currency, a fired bullet, and sample of dust and debris

5. At least three discharged cartridge cases; two may or may not have been fired by the same weapon

Procedure

Part I: Stereomicroscope

Review the diagram of a stereomicroscope (Figure 4.2). Note the two distinct optical systems by viewing the sample at approximately a 15-degree angle of divergence. This feature gives stereomicroscope samples their unique three-dimensional appearance .

The lab instructor will explain how to turn on the illuminator (be careful not to over-power the bulb). Focus the microscope, adjust it for your interpupillary distance, and correct for differences in diopter of your left and right eyes.

Optional Exercise: Calibration and Calculation

If your microscope is equipped with an eyepiece scale, calibrate its projected dimensions at low (10×) and projected high magnification (30×) by viewing the standard (stage micrometer or quality millimeter scale) under the microscope and aligning the eyepiece scale with the standard scale (see Figure 4.1). Count the stage micrometer units (SMUs) and ocular micrometer units (OMUs) between the two aligned marks on each scale. Fill in the data in Table 4.1. Calculate the projected dimension of each eyepiece scale unit at the desired magnification (value in fifth column).

TABLE 4.1

MAG ×	# SMU	# OMU	SMU SIZE PER DIVISION	# SMU × SIZE # OMU

Part II: Stereomicroscope Observations

The instructor will supply you with a number of items to view under the microscope. If possible, view them at low and high magnifications. Record your observations below. Prepare a sketch and label it appropriately. If you calibrated your eyepiece reticle, include measurements with your observations.

Observe a discharged bullet or other item that has a textured surface under lighting originating from different directions. This can be done by keeping the light stationary and rotating the sample or by keeping the sample in one position and moving the light source around the periphery. The angle of the light from the horizontal should also be varied if possible. The light should be placed at a very high angle, almost vertical to the surface observed, at least for a short time. Record your observations below.

Part III: Comparison of Firing Pin Impressions

You will be supplied with at least three discharged cartridge cases. Two or more may have been fired from the same weapon. They will have some identifying markings. View them under the microscope at an appropriate and comfortable magnification. Record your observations below. Make drawings if appropriate and note measurements. Determine, based on your observations, whether any of the casings were fired from the same weapon. These types of observations and determinations are in reality aspects of tool mark examination and the same principles of correlating tool and substrate apply. See Figure 4.3.

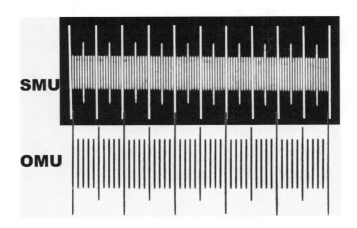

Figure 4.1
Superimposed image of stage micrometer (SM) aligned with image of ocular micrometer (OM). The SM covers 1 mm divided into 100 equal divisions, thereby making each unit (SMU) equal to 10 μm. The OM is divided into 50 equal units. The value for each OM unit must be determined by calibration with the SM.

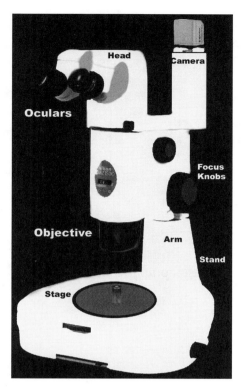

Figure 4.2
Stereomicroscope with shell casing on stage.

Figure 4.3
Macrophotograph of firing pin impression with image of ocular micrometer superimposed over primer cap.

Report

1. Report below the results of the eyepiece scale calibration if performed.

2. Report the results of cartridge case comparison.

3. Write a short narrative of what you learned in this experiment.

4. How does the image obtained with the stereomicroscope differ from the image obtained with the compound microscope?

Fingerprinting: Obtaining and Classifying Inked Prints and Lifting Latent Prints

Purposes

This experiment has two parts. First, each student will obtain an inked fingerprint set from another member of the class and attempt to classify each print according to its major group, thus learning how law enforcement personnel obtain reference fingerprints and classify them for future retrieval and identification.

The second part of the exercise involves location and preservation of a latent (invisible) fingerprint by powder dusting and tape lifting. The student will learn how crime scene personnel and investigators locate and preserve ridge impressions left at a crime scene for possible identification.

Equipment and Supplies

1. Fingerprint ink and roller with a piece of glass (about 9 × 18 in.) or other smooth surface on which to spread the ink
2. Fingerprint cards (Figure 5.4); magnifying glass (10× or more) or professional fingerprint examination glass with scale
3. Glass or ceramic containers (beakers or coffee cups) that can be dusted for latent prints.
4. Dark and light fingerprint powders or multipurpose powder with dusting brushes for both colors
5. Latent fingerprint lifting tape with backing material; hinged lifters (dark and light)
6. Fingerprint ink remover towelettes or paper towels, and waterless hand cleaner or denatured ethyl alcohol
7. Fingerprint dust safety hood for containing fine dust particles (optional)
8. Camera, preferably one capable of actual size one-to-one photography of fingerprints.

Procedure

1. Review the section on fingerprint classification in your textbook.

2. Obtain blank fingerprint cards, inking materials, and a magnifier from your instructor.

3. Prepare two fingerprint cards. Clearly print the names of the person to be printed and the person collecting the prints on one of the cards. Leave the second card blank. The collector will be graded on the quality of the prints submitted. Both students will be graded on their classifications of the prints.

4. Collect a set of rolled and plain inked prints from a fellow student.

5. Follow the instructions given by the instructor. Students usually achieve better results if the printer always stands to the left of the subject no matter which hand is being printed. The subject should stand behind the student who will obtain the print, about a forearm's length from the table. Carefully follow directions about whether prints should be rolled toward or away from the subject's body. Prints are usually ruined because too much rather than too little ink is used. Roll the ink out to a thin film on a smooth surface before use.

6. After printing is complete and cleaning of the subject's fingers and the printing station, classify the prints according to directions. The instructor may ask for the major classification or require more detail. Figure 5.1 shows arches, loops, and whorls. Figure 5.5 illustrates fingerprint characteristics. See also the appropriate chapter in your textbook. Record the results on the fingerprint cards and on fingerprint record on page 35. Use initials to indicate classification patterns (A = arch; L = loop; W = whorl). Use the following pattern configurations:

   Loops — Classified as ulnar or radial.

   Arches — Classified as plain or tented.

   Whorls — Classified as plain, double, central pocket, or accidental.

7. Obtain a latent dusting kit from the instructor. Make a few latent prints on a dark smooth surface, a light (white or ivory) surface, and on clear glass. Use a different finger for each surface. If you are unsuccessful in developing the print (making it visible), the reason may be that your fingers were too clean and dry. Repeat the exercise after touching your fingers to the side of your nose.

8. Choose an appropriate contrasting fingerprint dusting powder and the proper brush for its application. Brushes used with different powers are not interchangeable and will result in unsatisfactory prints. Tap or twirl the brush to remove any excess powder left from the last use. Figure 5.2 illustrates the technique of using white power to develop a latent print on a dark object.

9. Place a small amount of the powder into the jar cover or onto a piece of disposable paper. Dip the tips of the bristles into the powder. Clumping powder in the center bristles is considered poor practice because the clumping will deposit too much power and ruin the print. Using a circular sweeping motion, lightly brush across the area where the latent may be, then concentrate your action on the area where the print develops (becomes visible). Pick up a small amount of additional powder if required. Stop when development is complete. Too much brushing can destroy a print. Carefully remove excess powder with a clean brush.

10. Photograph the print, preferably 1:1 or life size.

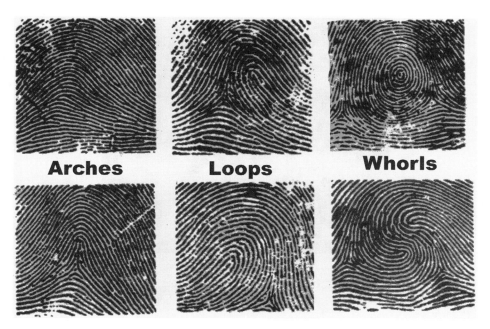

FIGURE 5.1
Basic fingerprint classification patterns.

FIGURE 5.2
The use of a feather duster with white powder to develop a latent fingerprint on a dark object.

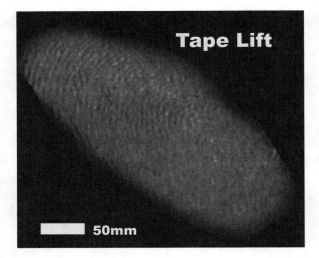

FIGURE 5.3
Latent print lifted with tape and placed on a black background.

11. Follow the directions of the lifter manufacturer to lift the print. Figure 5.3 shows a lifted latent print. The following are general directions.

   a. Open the lifter so that the arrow points to the upper right. Starting at the upper right, peel off the plastic cover and discard it. This exposes the adhesive.

   b. Place the tacky side of the lifter carefully over the latent image or print. Rub the plastic sheet lightly and thoroughly. Lift the powdered print. The star symbol should face you when you lift the print.

   c. The cover of the hinged lifter now protects the lifted print from scratches, damage, and dirt. To complete the lift, cover the lifted print by placing the lifter on its back (with the adhesive side up). Form a gentle curl with the backing cover and carefully roll the cover over the print lifter.

   d. The lifted print is now sealed. Any attempt to separate the backing and the lifter will result in damage or destruction of the lifted image. Keep the question mark facing you (face up) to ensure the print is a positive image; that is, it will appear as it did on the surface on which it was found. See Figure 5.3.

12. Classify the lifted prints to a major group. Classify them further if the instructor instructs you to do so. Record your results on the fingerprint record and tape the lifts to page 37.

13. Turn in the inked print card to the instructor. It may be photocopied. The original or a copy will be returned to you later. Paste the card to page 37 in this workbook after your instructor returns it to you.

14. Clean the work area and remove dusting powder and ink residues. Return materials to the instructor or to a predetermined area of the lab.

Fingerprint Record

Date_____

Name of person printed_____

Name of person collecting prints_____

Classification based on arches, loops, and whorls:

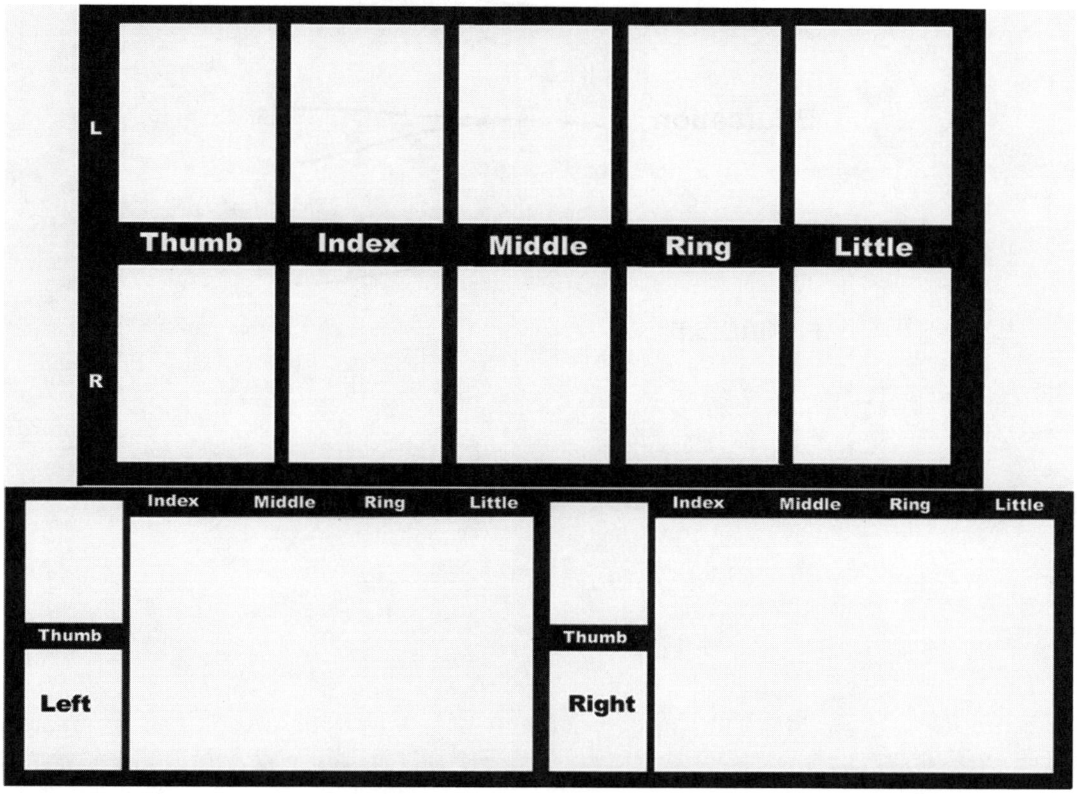

L				
Thumb	**Index**	**Middle**	**Ring**	**Little**
R				

	Index	Middle	Ring	Little		Index	Middle	Ring	Little
Thumb					**Thumb**				
Left					**Right**				

FIGURE 5.4

A Few Fingerprint Characteristics

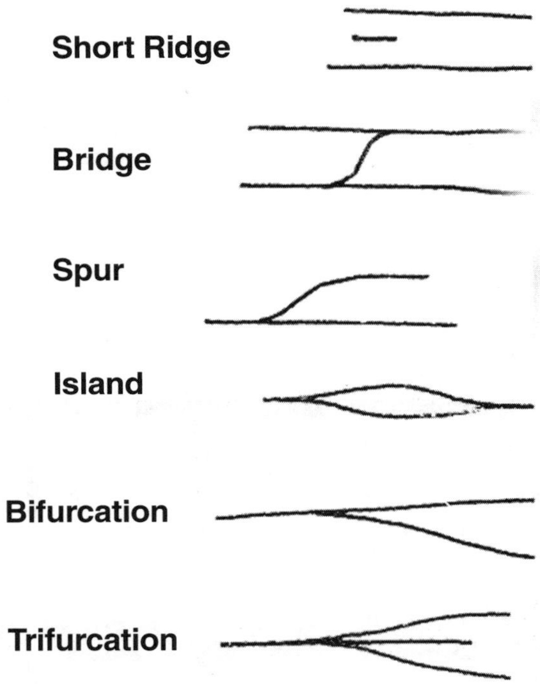

Short Ridge

Bridge

Spur

Island

Bifurcation

Trifurcation

FIGURE 5.5

Tape lifts here:

Tape fingerprint card here:

Report

1. Write a short narrative discussing what you learned in this exercise.

2. Describe skills you gained in preparing inked prints and in using lifting techniques to develop latent prints.

Identification and Matching of Fingerprints

Purpose

This experiment allows the student to identify and compare fingerprints.

Equipment and Supplies

1. Cards (prepared in Experiment 5) containing rolled fingerprints of known individuals to be used as standards for identification and comparison
2. Set of unknown fingerprints
3. Magnifying glass

Procedure

1. Obtain unknown prints and reference (comparison) prints in an envelope from your instructor.
2. Record the identification data (numbers and/or letters) of the known and unknown prints in the appropriate areas of the Report section.
3. Compare each unknown set of prints from the envelope to known comparison prints on the cards. All unknown prints should be identified or reported as "no reference found" (see Figures 6.1 through 6.3 and descriptions of features below).
4. Note in the Report section all matches of unknown and known prints. List at least 14 matching features in the Report section.
5. Return all prints to your instructor.

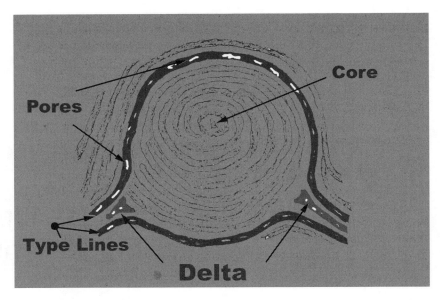

FIGURE 6.1
Examples of classification features.

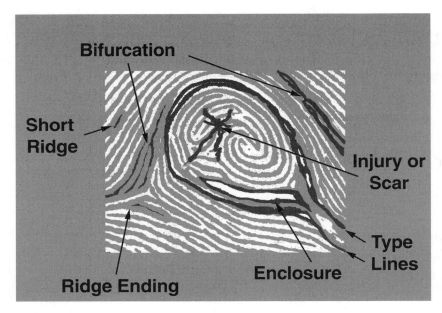

FIGURE 6.2
Examples of identifying features.

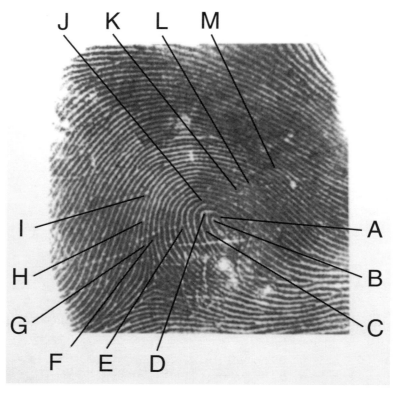

FIGURE 6.3
Fingerprint chart with identifying features, each designated by a letter.

Important Features and Descriptions

Bifurcation — Forking off of two friction ridges (see Figure 5.5 on page 36).

Core — Center of a loop, whorl, and some arch patterns.

Delta — Area of a ridge nearest the point of divergence of two type lines.

Friction Ridge Lines — Crests or high points of lines on the undersides of hands and feet. They are abundant and form unique patterns on the outer skin of fingers, palms, toes, and soles. Their troughs or low points are known as furrows.

Type Lines — Two ridges that run parallel to and surround the area of the fingerprint pattern.

Report

1. Record the identifications (numbers and/or letters) of the unknown fingerprints and next to it record the identifications (numbers and/or letters) of the reference (known) prints that match the unknown prints.

2. List at least 14 matching features of the unknown and known prints (see Figure 6.3):

(1) _____   (8) _____

(2) _____   (9) _____

(3) _____   (10) _____

(4) _____   (11) _____

(5) _____   (12) _____

(6) _____   (13) _____

(7) _____   (14) _____

7

Cyanoacrylate (Super Glue) Fuming for Fingerprint Development

Purpose

Learn to develop latent fingerprints on a plastic surface by cyanoacrylate (Super Glue) fuming. Implement safety precautions related to working near toxic fumes and using ultraviolet illumination.

Equipment and Supplies

1. Small item (provided by student) that can withstand fuming with Super Glue
2. Set of unknown fingerprints
3. Fuming chamber (an aquarium, 5 to 10 gallons, with a cover will suffice)*
4. Cyanoacrylate (Super Glue)
5. Cup warming plate
6. Aluminum cup
7. Beaker (100 mL) containing 50 mL water
8. Piece of clear plastic
9. Orange fluorescent dusting powder
10. Fiberglass dusting brush
11. Magnifying glass
12. Gloves
13. Safety glasses
14. Camera and film
15. Ultraviolet light

---

* An inexpensive chamber can be made from 4-mm thick plastic sheets. The chamber must be used inside a fume hood to contain toxic fumes.

Procedure

1. Place the item to be fumed in the fuming chamber along with a piece of plastic (control). The fuming chamber must be located under an exhaust hood or be connected to an external ventilation system. Figure 7.1 shows a typical arrangement for fuming a comb.

2. Place the beaker of water in the chamber.

3. Place the cup warming plate in the chamber.

4. Place the aluminum cup on top of the warming plate in the chamber.

5. Pour 2 mL of glue into the aluminum dish.

6. Close the door to the chamber as quickly as possible because the experiment will produce hazardous fumes.

7. Allow the fuming to proceed for 45 minutes. While the specimen is fuming, draw a sketch of the apparatus in the Report section on page 46.

8. After 45 minutes, slowly open the door of the chamber. This will allow the exhaust system to draw up the cyanoacrylate fumes.

9. Put on gloves and safety glasses. Examine the fumed item for latent prints (see Figure 7.2). Use oblique light if necessary.

10. Photograph the latent prints.

11. Dust the print with orange fluorescent dusting powder and examine it under the ultraviolet lamp. **NEVER LOOK INTO AN ULTRAVIOLET LAMP. IT PRODUCES RADIATION THAT WILL BURN YOUR EYES.**

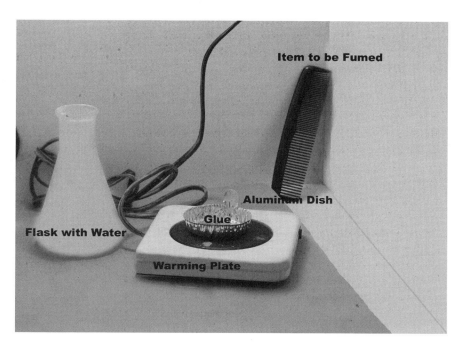

FIGURE 7.1
Fuming chamber for the Super Glue process.

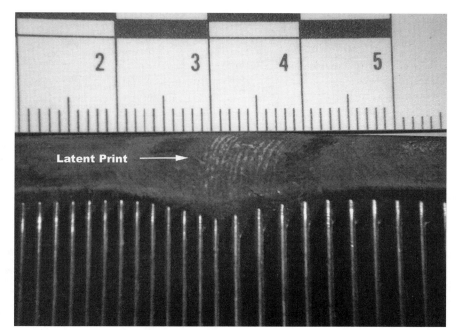

FIGURE 7.2
Fumed print on comb.

Report

1. Draw a sketch of the apparatus:

2. Record the results as directed by your instructor.

3. If possible, classify the latent print.

Crime Scene Investigation: Handling Evidence

Purpose

Introduce procedures for recognizing, finding, collecting, safeguarding, documenting, packaging, and preserving evidence found at crime scenes.

Equipment and Supplies

1. Mock crime scene
2. Diagram of mock crime scene (see Important Concepts and Observations, and Crime Scene Activities sections below)
3. Videocamera with tape
4. Still (35 mm) camera, film, flash, and other required accessories
5. Measuring devices: ruler, tape measure, protractor, compass
6. Protective clothing
7. Crime scene tape
8. Evidence searching equipment
9. Evidence collection and packaging supplies (envelopes, plastic containers, etc.)

Procedure

One student will be chosen for the role of first officer at the scene. Two students will serve as investigation detectives. Two will serve as emergency medical personnel. One student will act as medical examiner. Two will act as crime scene technicians assigned to process the scene. One student will be a forensic scientist called to the scene to assist with processing. Two students will act as reporter and cameraperson for the news media. The remaining students will act as witnesses, nonessential police personnel, and bystanders.

1. Based on the requirements of the role assigned to you, discuss the procedure you would follow at the crime scene shown in Figure 8.1. For example, emergency medical personnel would be concerned with the victim, not with processing evidence; a reporter might want to talk to the medical examiner, etc.

2. The instructor will direct an interactive dialogue with students in their assigned roles and discuss essential aspects of recognizing, finding, collecting, safeguarding, documenting, packaging, and preserving evidence found at crime scenes.

3. Process the prepared crime scene.

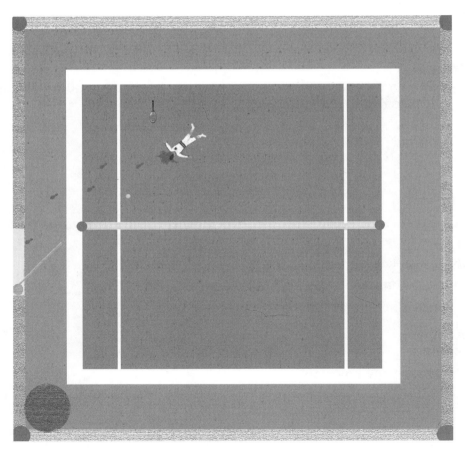

FIGURE 8.1

Important Concepts and Observations

Condition of victim; documentation

Medical treatment arranged if necessary

Note taking: who, what, when, where, why, how

Searching techniques: walk-through, walk-out

Search patterns: spiral, grid, wheel, zone

Measuring techniques: baseline, triangulation, polar coordinate, fixed point

Crime scene documentation

Crime scene diagram (including key, scale, legend, conditions, etc.)

Crime scene security

Exit of nonessential personnel, bystanders, etc.

Evidence handling

Crime Scene Activities

1. Walk-through (WT): A prompt and moderately slow walk through the crime scene by assigned officers (AOs). The WT starts at the outer limits of the crime scene and proceeds toward the seat of the crime. The intent is to obtain a quick overview of the physical evidence (PE). See Figure 8.2.

2. Suggested methods of searching for physical evidence at crime scenes:

   A. **Spiral method:** Start the WT at the outer borders of the scene and continue in a spiral pattern toward the seat of the crime, or start at the center of the spiral (seat) and proceed to the outer limits of the scene.

   B. **Wheel method:** Start at the seat of the crime and walk away from the seat along equal-length radial lines. Return to the center via the same radial line. See Figure 8.3.

   C. **Zonal method:** Divide the crime scene into small sectors or zones, and search each one individually. This method is effective for large area searches or vehicle searches. See Figure 8.4.

3. All physical evidence located during a search should be collected, documented, and vigilantly protected by trained personnel.

4. Documentation of crime scene and physical evidence:

   A. The pristine crime scene should be recorded by the videographer who should accompany an AO on the initial WT.

   B. Overall and specific photographs should be taken of the crime scene.

   C. Close-up (examination quality) photographs should be taken of important items of evidence, e.g., footwear impressions. The largest photographic format available should be employed for close-ups. The print image should fill the entire frame. A ruler should appear in the photograph to clearly show scale. A tripod should be used to hold the camera in a horizontal position. A level should be available to help properly position the camera.

D. Precise measurements of the crime scene and descriptive notes must be made. The notes should include an accurate sketch containing a key, a scale, and a legend noting the date, time, location, and conditions (weather, lighting, etc.). Compass directions should be noted on the sketch. See Figures 8.5 and 8.6.

E. A formal sketch should be prepared as soon as practicable from the rough sketch and descriptive notes generated at the scene.

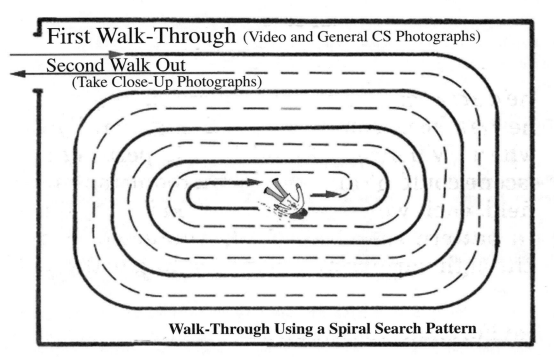

First Walk-Through (Video and General CS Photographs)

Second Walk Out
(Take Close-Up Photographs)

Walk-Through Using a Spiral Search Pattern

FIGURE 8.2

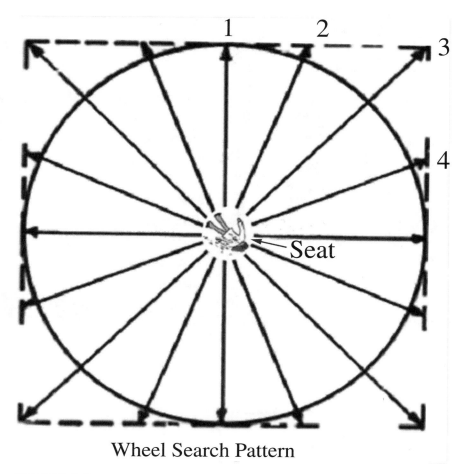

Wheel Search Pattern

FIGURE 8.3

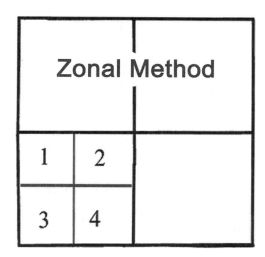

FIGURE 8.4

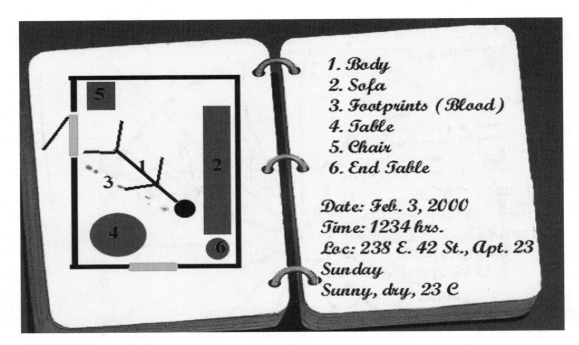

FIGURE 8.5

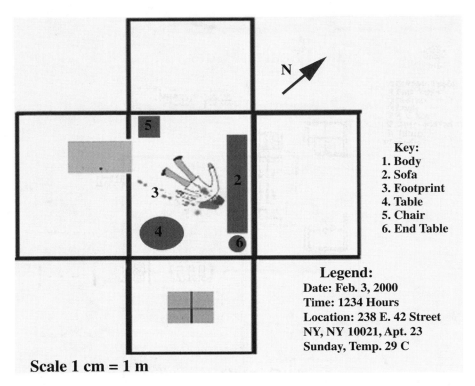

Scale 1 cm = 1 m

FIGURE 8.6

Report

1. List procedures for processing the prepared crime scene. Note all do's and don'ts.

2. Write an extensive report discussing processing of the prepared crime scene. The report should be prepared as if you would later use it to testify in court.

3. Write a formal critique of what was done correctly and what was done improperly at the crime scene. How do you think the scene should have been processed?

Experiment 9

Trace Evidence Collection

Purpose

Learn to collect trace materials from clothing items. package them, seal them, and mark them for identification. Remove trace evidence for examination and examine tape lifts under a stereomicroscope. Establish chain of custody and learn its importance to our legal system.

Equipment and Supplies

1. Roll of 2-inch clear lifting tape
2. Several pieces of clear plastic
3. Tweezers
4. Packaging containers
5. Stereomicroscope
6. Magnifying glass
7. Ultraviolet light
8. Items of clothing supplied by instructor
9. Large clean sheets of paper
10. Large table
11. Evidence storage cabinet

Procedure

1. Clean table top with water and paper towels.
2. Cover the tabletop with a sheet of clean paper.
3. Remove a clothing item from the evidence bag; place it on the prepared tabletop.

4. Sketch the item in No. 1 of the Report section.

5. Carefully look at all parts of the item. Remove all visible fibrous materials and store them in paper folds as demonstrated by your instructor. Note the locations of the visible fibrous materials.

6. Examine the clothing with the ultraviolet lamp. **CAUTION: NEVER LOOK INTO AN ULTRAVIOLET LAMP. THE RADIATION WILL BURN OR DAMAGE YOUR EYES**. Note the locations of fluorescing fibrous materials. Remove them and place them in paper folds.

7. Place a sheet of clear plastic next to the clothing.

8. Remove 6-in. pieces of clear tape and gently tape all surfaces of the item of clothing.

9. Place the adhesive side of the tape down onto a clear plastic sheet. It should adhere to the plastic. Figure 9.1 shows examples of tape lifts.

10. After placing identifying notations onto each prepared evidence package, insert the packages into an appropriate-sized evidence envelope.

11. Seal, date, and initial the envelope. Write identifying information on it and give it to your instructor.

12. Your instructor will give you an envelope prepared by another student. Open it and remove the packages. Open each package and describe the contents in detail (No. 3 of the Report section).

13. Examine the evidence under the stereomicroscope. Sort the materials according to type: all hairs are to be placed in one container, all fibers in another container, etc. All containers should be sealed, marked with identifying data, and placed in the evidence cabinet. Complete a chain of custody form for the evidence.

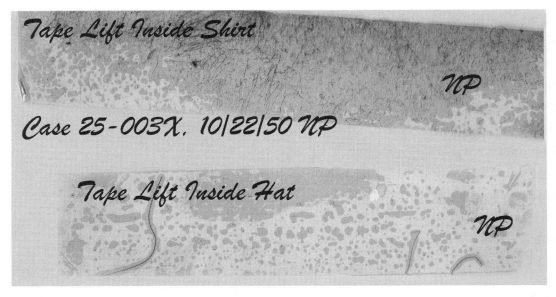

FIGURE 9.1
Tape lifts from clothing.

Chain of Custody Form

Evidence Control No. _____

Evidence received from _____

Time _____ Date _____

Evidence received by _____

Time _____ Date _____

Report

1. Sketch the item of clothing you examined.

2. Note on the above sketch the areas where fibers were found during visual examination. Note areas where fluorescing fibers were found.

3. Describe the items contained in the package your instructor gave you.

4. Write a complete report outlining your examination and observations.

5. Why is it important to mark the location of the fibrous evidence before it is removed from clothing?

6. Why is it important to mark for identification and seal fibrous evidence in a container?

7. Describe the chain of custody developed in this exercise.

8. Why is chain of custody important?

10

Sample Preparation for Microscopic Examination

Purpose

Introduce some of the methods and techniques used to prepare specimens for light microscopy examination and comparison.

Equipment and Supplies

1. Known tufts of hair and fiber specimens
2. Glass microscope slides and cover glasses
3. Assorted mounting media
4. Tweezers
5. Pencil with eraser
6. Filter paper
7. Hot plate
8. Rinzl®-brand plastic microscope slides (3 in. × 1 in. × 0. 5 mm)
9. Heavy-duty thread, 12-in. length
10. Size 5/10 sewing needle
11. Several new Teflon®-coated, single-edged razor blades
12. Light microscope

Procedure

Hair and fiber examinations are conducted every day in most forensic science laboratories around the globe. The samples must be properly singled out and prepared before they can be examined under a light microscope.

Preparation of Wet Mount in Cargille™* Permount® (Figure 10.1)

1. Single out the specimen to be prepared for examination.
2. Place a clean microscope slide on a piece of clean filter paper.
3. Place several drops of Permount on the microscope slide.
4. Place the specimen to be mounted on top of the resin.
5. Place a cover glass with a drop of Permount on its underside onto the specimen.
6. Gently press down with a pencil eraser to remove all the bubbles.
7. Label the slide and observe the scale impression with the microscope at 100×.

Preparation of Scale Cast in Cargille™ Melt Mount® (Figure 10.2)

1. Single out the specimen to be prepared for examination.
2. Adjust a hot plate to 60 to 70°C (the melting range of Melt Mount 1.539).
3. Place a clean microscope slide on the hot plate and gently warm it.
4. Apply a Melt Mount stick to the slide surface.
5. Use a fresh slide to spread the liquefied resin evenly across the slide containing the Melt Mount.
6. Remove the slide from the hot plate and allow it to cool for 30 seconds.
7. Place the hair to be cast on top of the Melt Mount and reheat the slide on the hot plate until the resin liquefies, about 5 seconds. Be sure the entire length of the hair is enclosed by the resin.
8. Remove the slide from the hot plate and allow it to cool completely.
9. Gently peel the hair from the slide. An impression of the hair will remain in the resin.
10. Observe the scale impression with the microscope at 100×.

---

* Permount and Melt Mount are registered trademarks of Cargille Laboratories, Inc., Cedar Grove, NJ.

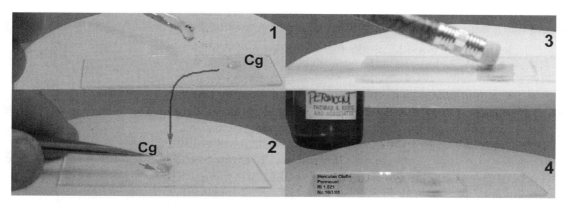

FIGURE 10.1
Preparation of a wet mount in Permount oil.

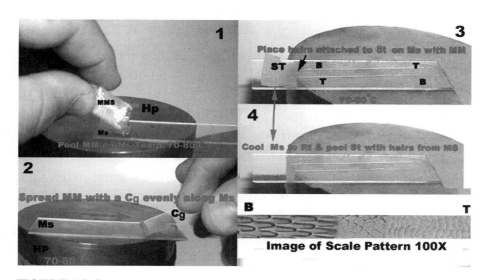

FIGURE 10.2
A method for the preparation of scale casts in Melt Mount 1.539.

Preparation of Wet Mount in Melt Mount (Figure 10.3)

1. Single out a hair or fiber to be mounted; you can use the hair that was just cast in Melt Mount.
2. Place a clean microscope slide on the hot plate and gently warm.
3. Apply a Melt Mount stick to the slide surface.
4. Spread the liquefied resin evenly across the microscope slide with a cover glass.
5. Place a drop of warmed resin on the underside of the cover glass.
6. Place the specimen to be mounted on top of the warm resin.
7. Softly place the cover glass on top of the preparation. Lightly press down on the cover glass with a pencil eraser to remove all the air bubbles.
8. Label the preparation, and observe the scale impression with the microscope at 100×.

Preparation of Hair or Fiber Cross Sections in Plastic Slides (Figure 10.4)

1. Single out tufts of hair or fibers to be cross-sectioned.
2. Double thread the needle with the length of heavy thread.
3. Use the needle to puncture a 1.0 mm hole into the center of a plastic slide.
4. Draw the needle completely through the plastic slide, leaving a loop of thread on the opposite side of the slide. Remove the needle.
5. Place a bundle of the hairs or fibers to be cross-sectioned into the loop of thread. Pull the thread downward until the bundle of hair or fibers is drawn halfway through the slide.
6. Leave equal parts of the bundle on both sides of the slide.
7. Cut the hair or fiber bundle with a new razor blade. Hold the cutting edge of the blade at about a 30-degree angle to the surface of the slide as you draw the blade across the slide surface. Cut the hair or fiber material flush to both sides of the slide.
8. Use the light microscope to view the hair or fibrous material directly or after mounting it in an appropriate mounting medium.

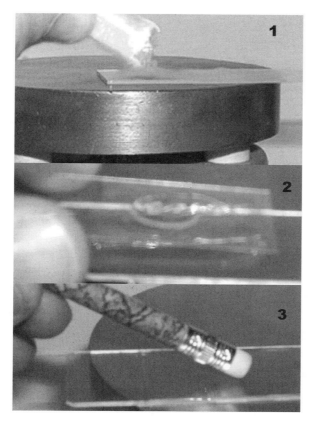

FIGURE 10.3
Preparation of wet mount in Melt Mount.

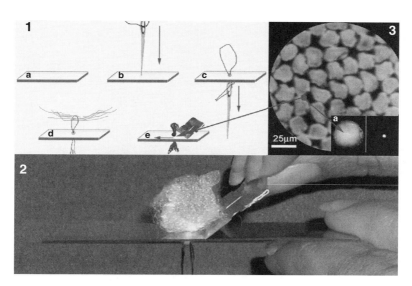

FIGURE 10.4
The cross sectioning of fibrous materials with plastic microscope slides.

Report

1. Describe the appearances of all the specimens you prepared for the laboratory.

2. Tape all the prepared slides to this page.

Experiment 11

Examination of Human Hair

Purposes

Introduce the student to techniques for mounting, examining, and characterizing human hair and provide additional training in light microscopy.

Equipment and Supplies

1. Questioned hair specimens collected in Experiment 9
2. Glass microscope slides and cover glasses
3. Mounting media
4. Tweezers
5. Pencil with eraser
6. Filter paper
7. Light microscope

Procedure

Forensic hair examinations provide important investigative and associative information. Human hair has been used in forensic investigations for nearly a century. The basis for microscopic identification and comparison of human hair is its morphology. Figure 11.1 illustrates basic features examined during a microscopic hair comparison. Figures 11.2 through 11.4 are labeled photomicrographs of human hair. The glossary below defines common terms used in hair examination. Table 11.1 is a protocol designed to help you determine which features of hair to examine.

1. Pull a hair from your head and mount it in Permount® using the technique described in Experiment 10.

2. Examine it under the light microscope at 40× and 100× magnification.

3. Prepare a hair data sheet (Report section) for your specimen. The data sheet lists parameters that will help you determine certain somatic and other identification and comparison characteristics.

4. Review your findings with your instructor.

5. Use Permount to mount one of the questioned hairs collected in Experiment 9.

6. Prepare a hair data sheet for the questioned specimen.

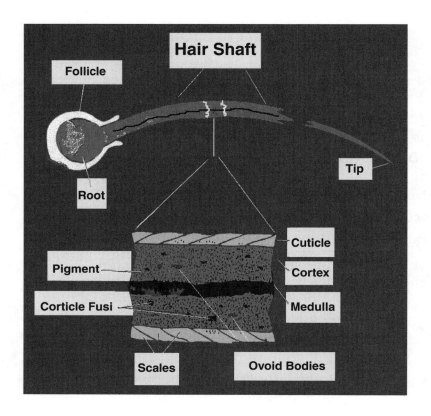

FIGURE 11.1

A court diagram used to show some of the basic physical features examined during a microscopic hair comparison.

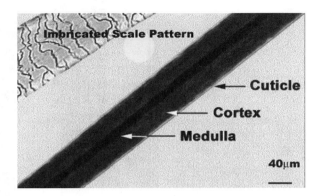

FIGURE 11.2

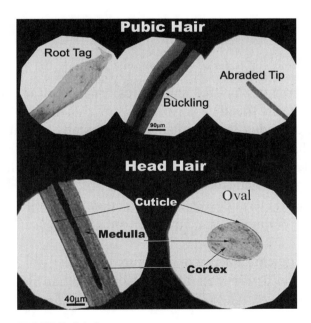

FIGURE 11.3

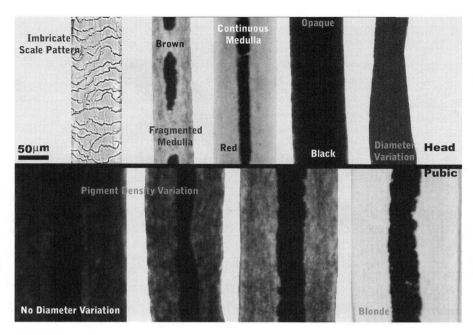

FIGURE 11.4

Glossary of Hair Terms

Anagen phase — Active growth phase of hair follicle. A root of an anagen hair is elongated, pigmented, and may have a sheath.

Buckling — Appearance of caving in of the hair shaft; normally present in pubic hair.

Catagen phase — Step-down phase of hair growth. The period between active growth (anagen phase) and resting (telogen phase). A catagen root may be club-shaped and may contain a meager amount of pigment and a dried root sheath.

Caucasoid — Anthropological term designating the people of Europe.

Cellular — Displaying a definite form, pattern, or shape; usually refers to medullary configuration.

Characteristic — Microscopic or macroscopic feature of a hair.

Color — Hue or shade of hair determined under reflected and transmitted light.

Comparison — Examination of questioned and known hair specimens to associate or disassociate them from a given individual.

Cortex — Primary anatomical part of a hair between the cuticle and medullary regions.

Cortical fusi — Small spaces within hair shafts that appear as tiny dark specks.

Cross-sectional shape — Shape of a hair shaft when cut at right angles to its longitudinal axis.

Cuticle — Outermost region of a hair; composed of layers of overlapping scales.

Distal end — End of a hair farthest from the root.

Hair — Fine, cylindrically shaped fiber growing from the skin of mammals.

Imbricate — Scale pattern whose edges overlap in a wavy pattern.

Keratin — Fibrous, sulfur-containing protein that forms the chemical basis for keratinized epidermal tissue such as hair.

Known sample — A sample intended to be representative of a particular body area of a specific person or animal.

Macroscopic — Large enough to be perceived by the unaided human eye or under low magnification.

Medial region — Part of a hair between the proximal and distal ends.

Medulla — Center of the cortex.

Medullary configuration — Form of a medullary cell from the proximal end to the distal end of the hair shaft.

Melanin — Pigment that provides hair color.

Mongoloid — Anthropological designation for human beings from Asia and including the Inuit peoples and the Amerindians.

Negroid — Anthropological term designating the peoples of Africa.

Ovoid bodies — Oval or round pigmented bodies usually found in hair cortex.

Pigment density — Relative abundance of pigment granules in hair cortex, determined by their microscopic appearance.

Pigment distribution — Pattern of pigment granules about the central axis of the hair shaft (uniform, peripheral, one-sided, random, central).

Proximal end — End of a hair nearest the root.

Questioned sample — Sample of unknown origin.

Regional origin — Originating from one of three major groups of humans (see **Caucasoid, Mongoloid,** and **Negroid**).

Root — Structure at the proximal end of a hair that extends from the follicle.

Scales — Tiny plate-like structures made of keratin; intended to protect hairs.

Telogen phase — Final phase of hair growth cycle; the root assumes a bulbous shape that can be easily shed from a follicle.

Tip — Most distal end of a hair shaft vulnerable to effects of bleaching and mechanical damage.

TABLE 11.1
Protocol for Determining Hair Characteristics

A. Microscopic Characteristics

Color:

____Colorless ____Blonde ____Red ____Brown ____Black ____Other

Natural Pigment:

Size: ____Fine ____Coarse

Aggregation: ____Streaky ____Clumpy ____Patchy

Aggregate Size: ____Small ____Medium ____Large

Density: ____Sparse ____Medium ____Heavy ____Opaque

Distribution: ____Uniform ____Peripheral ____One-sided ____Random ____Other

Treatment: ____Dye ____Rinse ____Bleach ____Spray dye ____Coating dye ____Lightener ____Other

Shaft:

Diameter range: ____to ____μm

Shape: ____Round ____Oval ____Triangular ____Oblate ____Other

Configuration: ____Buckled ____Convoluted ____Shouldered ____Invaginated ____Undulated ____Split ____Regular

B. Anatomical Regions and Their Characteristics

Medulla: ____Present ____Absent ____Continuous ____Discontinuous ____Fragmented ____Opaque ____Translucent ____Amorphous ____Cellular ____Other (e.g., doubled)

Cuticle: ____Present ____Absent

Outer Cuticle Margin: ____Flattened ____Smooth ____Serrated ____Cracked ____Looped ____Other

Inner Cuticle Margin: ____Distinct ____Indistinct ____Other

Cortex: ____Cellular texture ____Coarse ____Medium ____Fine

Ovoid Bodies: ____Size ____Distribution ____Abundance

Cortical Fusi: ____Size ____Shape ____Distribution

Distal End: ____Tapered ____Abraded ____Square cut ____Angular cut ____Frayed ____Split ____Crushed ____Broken ____Burned ____Other

Proximal End: ____No root ____Anagen ____Catagen ____Telogen ____Root tag ____Root band ____Skeletal

Report

Human Hair Data Sheet

Color _____

Length _____

Shape _____

Texture _____

Cuticle _____

Cortex _____

Tip _____

Pigment distribution _____

Pigment density _____

Medullary structure _____

Root shape _____

Growth phase _____

Human Hair Data Sheet

Color _____

Length _____

Shape _____

Texture _____

Cuticle _____

Cortex _____

Tip _____

Pigment distribution _____

Pigment density _____

Medullary structure _____

Root shape _____

Growth phase _____

1. Document the correct procedures for microscopic examination of human hair.

2. Sketch your head hair specimen.

3. Sketch your questioned hair specimen.

4. Make a list of the characteristics of each specimen. How do the specimens differ? How are they the same?

Experiment 12

Examination of Mammalian Hair

Purpose

Introduce the student techniques for mounting, examining, and characterizing nonhuman mammalian hair and provide additional training in light microscopy.

Equipment and Supplies

1. Questioned hair specimens collected in Experiment 9
2. Glass microscope slides and cover glasses
3. Mounting media, including Cargille™ Melt Mount® 1.539
4. Hot plate
5. Known animal hair standards
6. Fine tweezers
7. Pencil with eraser
8. Filter paper
9. Light microscope

Procedure

Animal hairs are often encountered in forensic casework. Hairs shed by domestic pets, such as cats, dogs, ferrets, and hamsters, are often found on clothing items or in dust specimens. Pet hairs are carried into interior environments. Animal hairs originating from articles of clothing (e.g., fur hats) and other manufactured items can become airborne and adhere to dust inside buildings and vehicles. Animal hairs used in manufacturing textiles and carpets are easily transferred among people, places, and things. The investigative information provided by animal hair evidence is often used to help associate people with crimes, to reconstruct crimes, and ultimately to solve crimes.

1. Use fine tweezers to remove suspected animal hair collected from the clothing examined in Experiment 9 from the tapes, paper folds, or storage containers. If necessary to aid removal, view the fabric under a stereomicroscope or magnifying glass.

2. Prepare scale casts of suspected animal hair specimens by following the procedure explained in Experiment 10.

3. After removal from the casting resin (Step 3), mount the hairs in Melt Mount 1.539 as explained in Experiment 10.

4. Examine the hair specimens under 40× and 100× magnification.

5. Prepare an animal hair data sheet (Report section) for each specimen.

6. Compare the questioned specimens with the specimens depicted in the four figures included in this section and known animal hair specimens provided by your instructor. Figure 12.1 shows petal-shaped scale configurations. Figure 12.2 shows wavy and chevron-shaped scale configurations. Figure 12.3 shows medullary configurations. Figure 12.4 shows the construction of guard hairs.

7. Attempt to identify the unknown animal with the aid of the Figure 12.5 flow chart.

8. Review your findings with your instructor.

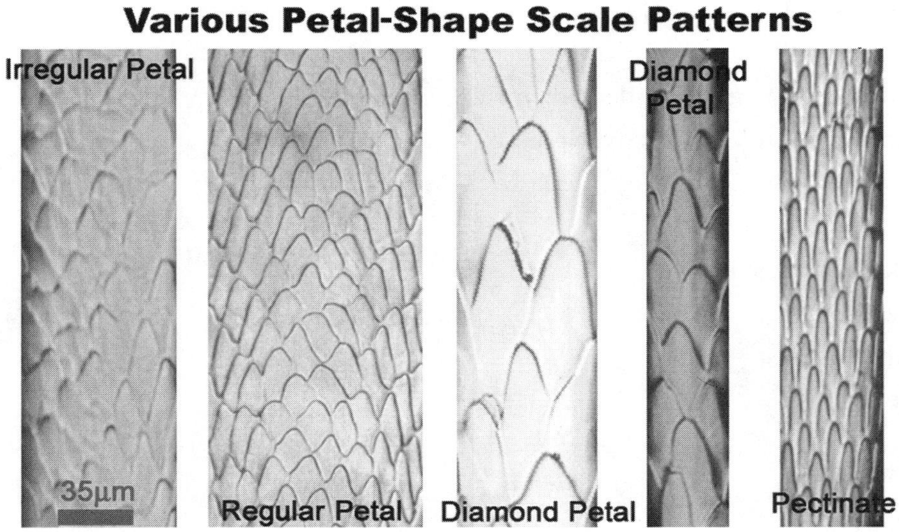

Various Petal-Shape Scale Patterns

FIGURE 12.1
Various petal-shaped scale pattern configurations.

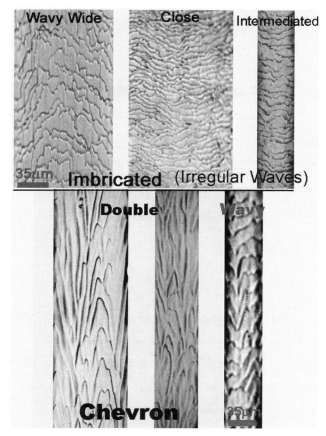

FIGURE 12.2
Various wavy- and chevron-shaped scale patterns.

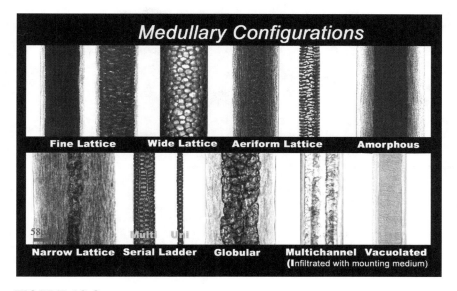

FIGURE 12.3
Various medullary configurations.

81

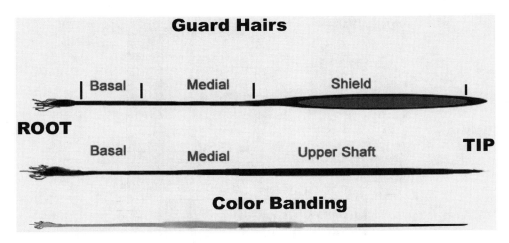

FIGURE 12.4

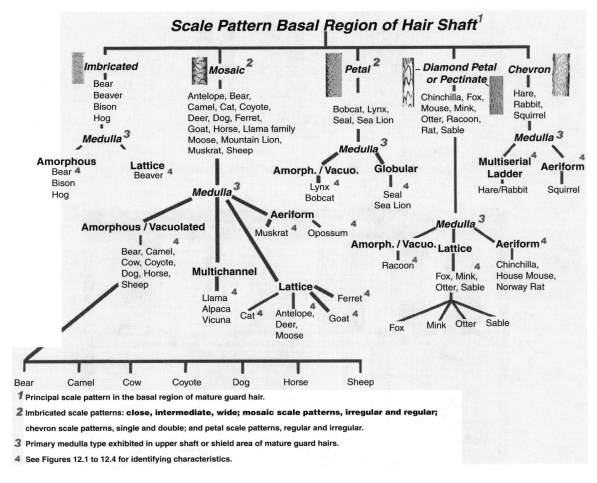

FIGURE 12.5

Report

1. Document the correct procedures for microscopic examination of animal hair.

2. Sketch your animal hair specimen. Draw the three primary anatomical structures: cortex, medulla, cuticle.

3. List the characteristics used to identify each species of animal hair.

Animal Hair Data Sheet

Cortex

Shape of hair: _____ Straight _____ Curly _____ Wavy

Length of Shaft in mm _____

Maximum _____ Minimum _____ Average _____

Color: _____ Reflected _____ Transmitted

Single color _____ Multicolored_____

Banded _____
(Describe banding from tip end to root.)

Pigment density and distribution _____
(e.g., heavy, toward cuticle)

Shaft diameter (μm) _____

Root shape _____

Tip shape _____

Medulla

Medulla: _____ Absent _____ Present

Medullary configuration _____

Changes along shaft _____
(Describe from tip to root end.)

Medullary index: _____ Diameter of medulla _____ Diameter of shaft

Cuticle

Scale patterns along shaft _____
(Describe from tip to root end.)

13

Microscope Measurements

Purposes

Introduce light microscopy measurement procedures. The student will gain experience in manipulating and mounting several types of fibrous and particulate specimens into different media and obtain further experience using a light microscope for identification.

Equipment and Supplies

1. Questioned specimens collected in Experiment 9
2. Ocular and stage micrometers (your microscope may be equipped already with an ocular micrometer; follow your instructor's directions)
3. Glass microscope slides and cover glasses
4. Assorted mounting media
5. Known synthetic fiber standards
6. Fine tweezers
7. Filter paper
8. Pencil with eraser
9. Light microscope

Procedure

Measurement of small linear distances, angles, and areas with a microscope is known as micrometry. Quantitative measurement with a microscope involves the use of various types of ocular scales, some of which are calibrated with a stage micrometer. The normal unit of measurement for length, width, and thickness is the micrometer (abbreviated as μm). One μm equals one millionth of a meter or 10^{-6} m.

Two types of micrometers are used with microscopes. The first is the ocular micrometer (OCM) — usually an arbitrary scale on a round glass disc placed at the primary focal plane of the ocular. Ocular scales have many configurations: (1) a small horizontal or vertical ruler divided into 100 equal divisions, (2) a cross-hair combining vertical and horizontal rulers, (3) a grid divided into 100 equal squares. The second type is the stage micrometer (SM). This is typically a scale of known length, normally 1 mm, divided into 100 equal divisions. Each division value equals 10 µm. See Figure 13.1.

1. Position the OCM into the eyepiece as depicted in Figure 13.2.

2. To determine the value of each ocular micrometer unit (OMU), align the image of the SM with the image of the OCM (Figure 13.3). Both micrometers are aligned as a vernier. The OMUs and stage micrometer units (SMUs) are counted and recorded. The value in micrometers for 1 OMU equals the number of SMUs times the value for each SMU divided by the number of OMUs.

3. Follow this procedure for each objective lens. Record the value for each objective in the Report section and on a piece of tape attached to the base of your microscope for quick reference. This value will not change as long as the objectives, oculars, body tube, and head are not changed. Figure 13.4 shows microscope images generated when a 20× objective was calibrated. Figure 13.5 depicts the measurement of a human head hair cross section with a calibrated OCM.

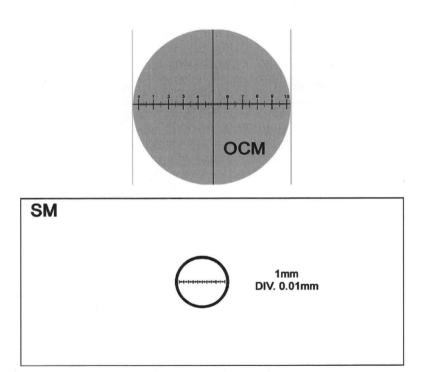

FIGURE 13.1
Two common types of micrometer scales: the ocular micrometer (top) and the stage micrometer (bottom).

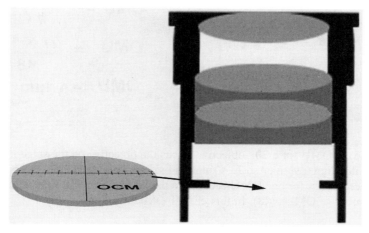

FIGURE 13.2
Placement of the ocular micrometer into the eyepiece.

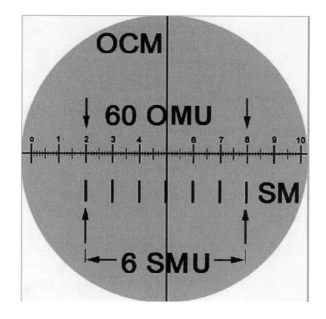

FIGURE 13.3
Top: A typical ocular micrometer (OCM). Bottom: A stage micrometer (SM). Calibration of an OCM is shown. To determine the value for each ocular micrometer unit (OMU), align the image of the SM with the OCM and count and record the number of OMUs and stage micrometer units (SMUs).

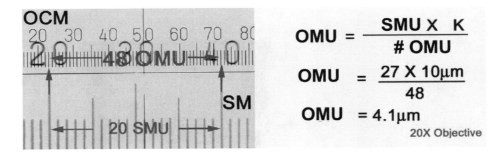

FIGURE 13.4

To determine the value for each OMU for a 20× objective, focus the objective on the stage micrometer. Align the OCM and SM images as you would align a vernier scale. Count and record the number of OMUs and SMUs that align with each other. The value in micrometers for one OMU is equal to the number of SMUs (20) times the value for each SMU (10 μm) divided by the number of OMUs (48). In this case, 1 OMU = 4.1 μm.

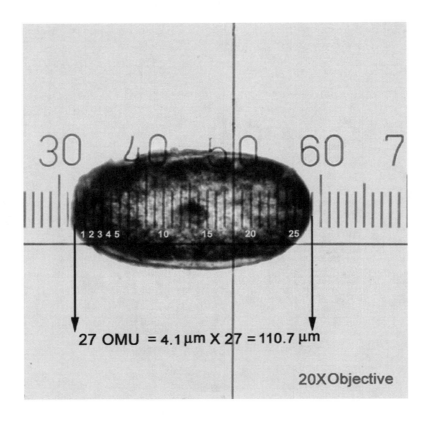

FIGURE 13.5

Measurement of a human head hair cross section (X-S) with the calibrated OCM and 20× objective combination shown in Figure 13.4. To determine the hair's width, the image of the hair should be aligned with the OCM units. The number of OMUs that align with the hair X-S are counted and recorded. The value in micrometers for the hair X-S is equal to the number of OMUs (27) times the value for each unit (4.1 μm). In this case, the hair X-S equals 27 × 4.1 μm or 110.7 μm.

Report

1. Document the correct procedures for calibration of an ocular micrometer with a stage micrometer.

2. Measure the thicknesses of five specimens: a hair, two fibers, and two specimens of your choice (e.g., pollen grains, mineral grains, yeast mold, plant materials, etc.). Document all measurements clearly and completely.

3. Calibrate all the objectives available on your microscope.

4. Prepare a table listing the values of one OMU for each objective lens calibrated.

14

Examination of Synthetic Fibers

Purpose

Introduce procedures for the examination, mounting, and characterization of synthetic fibers and further work with light microscopy.

Equipment and Supplies

1. Questioned fiber specimens collected in Experiment 9
2. Glass microscope slides and cover glasses
3. Mounting media: Cargille™ Melt Mount® 1.539 or high density oil
4. Known synthetic fiber standards
5. Fine tweezers
6. Pencil with eraser
7. Filter paper
8. Light microscope

Procedure

Synthetic fibers are often encountered in forensic casework. They are found in wearing apparel, draperies, textiles, and carpets, and are easily transferred among people, places, and things. The investigative information provided by fiber evidence is often used to help associate people with locations, help reconstruct events, and help solve crimes.

One must clearly see a specimen in order to collect fundamental information about its appearance or physical structure. The extent to which a colorless to lightly colored transparent fiber can be seen when immersed in a colorless or nearly colorless mounting medium (MTM) is known as *relief*. If the specimen and the MTM have the same refractive index (RI), the specimen will not be visible when viewed with a polarizing light microscope (PLM) under plane polarized light (PPL). If the RI of the MTM is close to that of the specimen, low relief results. If the RI is somewhat different from that of the specimen, moderate relief can be observed and the specimen will be fairly visible in the MTM. If the difference between the specimen and MTM refractive indices is large, high relief will result and the specimen will appear to stand out of the MTM.

1. Use a fine tweezers to remove the suspected synthetic fibers collected in Experiment 9 from the tapes, paper folds, or containers in which they were stored. Observe them at low magnification under a stereomicroscope or use a magnifying glass.

2. Prepare a wet mount of the questioned fiber specimens collected in Experiment 9 by following the procedure outlined in Experiment 10. The mount should be prepared in a Cargille oil having an RI of approximately 1.540 at 25°C for the sodium D line (589 nm).

3. Enter fiber morphology observations on the fiber data sheet in the Report section.

    A. Note longitudinal appearance. Are the fibers smooth, serrated, round, square, pentagonal, lobed, or irregular? See Figure 14.1.

    B. If possible, determine the cross-sectional shapes of the fibers by their longitudinal appearance.

    C. Measure the diameter thickness of the fiber (μm) as instructed in Experiment 13.

4. Enter all fiber optical data on the data sheet included in the Report section. To determine whether a fiber is anisotropic (has more than one refractive index), place a polarizing light filter under the microscope condenser with its preferred vibration direction in the East-West position (left). As the fiber is observed at 100×, slowly rotate the filter until its preferred direction is in the North-South position. If the contrast between the fiber and the mounting appears to change as in Figure 14.2, the fiber is birefringent (has two or more RIs). If no change in the fiber appearance is noted, the fiber is isotropic (has one RI).

    A. Is the fiber easily visible in the mounting medium? What is its degree of relief? High relief fiber is distinctly visible; a low relief fiber image blends into the mounting medium.

    B. Does the fiber have more then one refractive index? See Figure 14.2. Is the fiber isotropic (having only one refractive index) or anisotropic (having more than one refractive index)?

    C. If the fiber is anisotropic, determine its relative refractive indices in the mounting medium by the Becke line method. See Figure 14.3.

    D. To determine the generic classification of an unknown fiber, the collected information on the fiber data sheet in the Report section is compared to the data in Table 14.1 and the flow chart (Figure 14.4).

    E. Identify each class of fiber specimen in the same manner. If a comparison of the fibers is desired, the questioned and known specimens can be compared side-by-side on a comparison microscope.

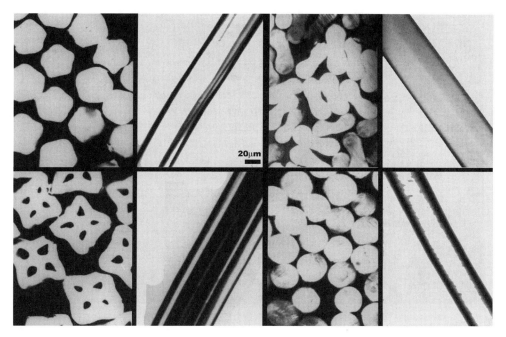

FIGURE 14.1
A few fiber cross-section shapes. Note their X-S shape and the corresponding longitudinal appearances.

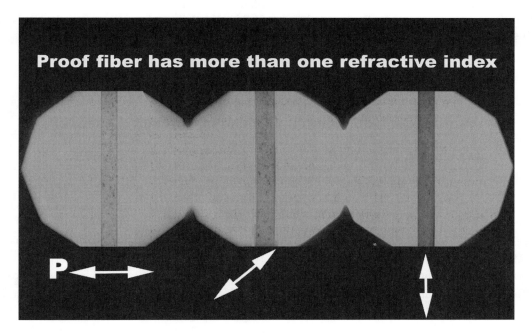

FIGURE 14.2
Fiber displaying a low relief condition (left) and a high relief condition (right).

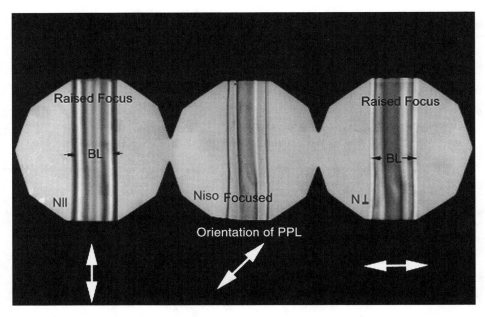

FIGURE 14.3

Determination of the relative refractive index (RRI) for NII and N⊥ directions. The procedure involves the observation of the Becke line movement in plane polarized light for both the NII and N⊥ orientations of the fiber. After focusing the specimen (center), the orientation of the polarizing filter is made parallel to the long direction of the fiber (NII). The microscope focus is then raised and the movement of the Becke line is noted (right). The orientation of the polarizing filter is then adjusted until its vibration direction is perpendicular to the width of the fiber (N⊥). The microscope focus is then raised and the movement of the Becke line is noted in this orientation (left). In this case, the NII is greater than the mounting medium (MTM), and the N⊥ is less than the MTM.

TABLE 14.1
Synthetic Fibers Commonly Seen in Forensic Casework

Generic Class	NII/N⊥ Relative Refractive Indices	Birefringence	Relief	X-S
Acrylic	Both < 1.539	Very low	Low–med.	Bean, dog bone, mushroom, round
Polyamide (nylon 6,6.6)	nII > 1.539 n⊥ < 1.539	High	Low–med.	Round, trilobal, tetralobal
Glass, mineral wool	Isotropic	None	Low	Round, off-round, irregular
Olefin (propylene)	(Range 1.510–620) Both < 1.539	Med.	Low–med.	Round, trilobal, delta, flat
Polyester	nII >> 1.539 n⊥ ~ 1.539	Very high	Low–high	Round, ovoid, polygonal, donut, trilobal, swollen ribbon

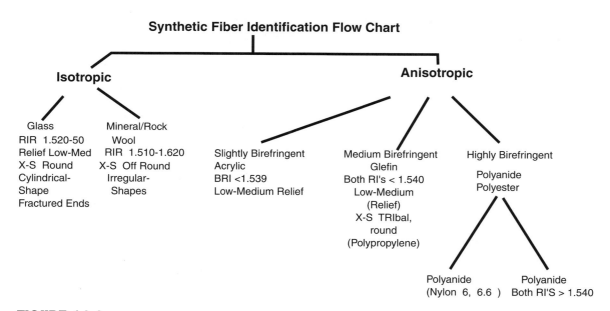

FIGURE 14.4

RIR — Refractive index range. BRI — Both refractive indices.

Report

1. Document the correct procedures for microscopic examination of synthetic fibers.

2. Sketch longitudinal and cross-section views of your fiber specimen.

3. List the characteristics used to identify each class of synthetic fiber.

Fiber Data Sheet

Part I: Fiber Morphology

Longitudinal morphology (circle one): smooth, striated, cross-hatched, irregular, other

Cross-sectional shape _____

Diameters of lobes (μm) _____

Reflected color _____

Transparency _____

Transmitted color _____

Length (mm) _____

Surface texture _____

Staple length or continuous _____

Coloration (circle one): pigment or organic dye

Treatment (circle one): twisted, crimped, melted

Presence, extent, and type of dulling agent _____

Other manufactured artifacts (gas bubbles, fish eyes, etc.) _____

Part II: Optical Data

Relative Rl (relative to medium 1.539 to 1.540 or another mounting medium with known RI):

    N parallel (NII)   above   below   near   equal to _____

    N perpendicular (N⊥) above   below   near   equal to _____

Using polarizer, is filter isotropic or anisotropic? _____

Interference colors: _____

UV fluorescence _____

Other information _____

Experiment 15

Basics of Photography

Purpose

Introduce the basics of traditional photography and operation of a 35-mm camera.

Equipment and Supplies

1. Camera (35 mm) with assorted lenses
2. Tripod or photographic stand, e.g., MP4
3. Different speeds (ISO) of 35-mm film
4. Different types of evidence displays
5. Scales

Procedure

1. Study the parts of a 35-mm camera (Figure 15.1 shows a top view of a camera) and the glossary terms on page 104.
2. Practice operating the camera as directed by your instructor.
3. Photograph the evidence displays using different lighting techniques.
4. Develop the film as instructed. If black-and-white film is used, refer to Experiment 16.
5. Some important concepts to consider:
   A. How a lens forms an image (Figure 15.2 shows formation of an image when light rays. enter a lens and are refracted or bent; converging rays form an inverted image).
   B. How a camera works (Figure 15.3 shows the basic elements of a 35-mm camera).
   C. Film speed (ISO).
   D. Film image size.

E. Focusing the image onto the film plane.

F. Coverage of the object area.

G. Size of aperture opening or f-stop.

H. Maximum depth of field obtainable.

I. Shutter speed or exposure time.

J. True size of object in print (scale).

K. Relationship between exposure time and f-stop — (EV) exposure value.

L. Working distance from object to front of lens.

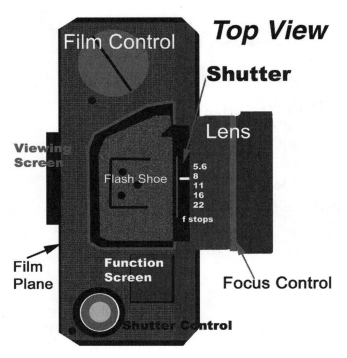

FIGURE 15.1
Top view of 35-mm camera.

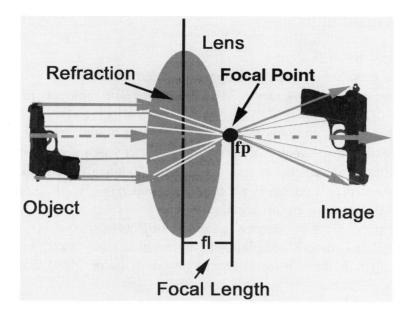

FIGURE 15.2

Formation of an image by a lens. An image is formed when rays of light traveling from an object enter a lens and are refracted or bent. The converging rays of bent light form an inverted real image of the object.

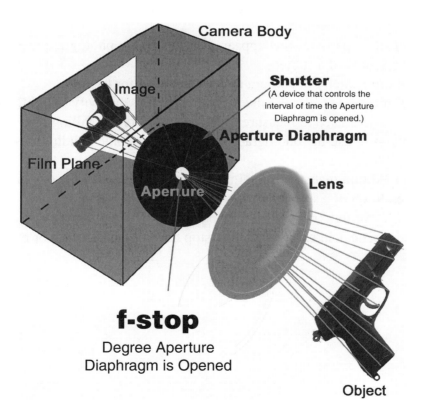

FIGURE 15.3

Depicted are the basic elements of a 35-mm camera.

103

Photography Glossary

Aberration — Optical defect in a lens.

Acetate — Cellulose acetate film base that supports film emulsion.

Aperture lens opening or f-stop — Device that regulates the amount of light entering a camera.

Bellows — Adjustable tube or chamber that connects the lens to the camera body.

Cable release — Flexible wire capable of activating a shutter when depressed.

Clearing agent — Solution that reduces washing time by chemically neutralizing fixing agents.

Contact print — Image produced when photographic paper is placed against a negative and controlled light passes through the negative.

Depth of field — Distance from the nearest to farthest objects in sharp focus in a photograph.

Emulsion — Thin gelatin coating containing light-sensitive silver salts; used to coat film or photographic paper. A manufacturer assigns an emulsion or speed value that determines proper exposure.

Fix — Dissolution of undeveloped silver salts on a film through the use of hypo (sodium thiosulfate).

Focal length — Distance from the center of the lens to the focal point.

Focus — Adjusting the lens to film distance in order to sharply define a subject.

f-stop — Designation indicating the aperture size (opening) and the amount of light passing into lens.

Grains — Clumped silver particles that appear as light spots in photographic prints.

Highlight — Brightest area of a subject.

Hypo — Bath consisting chiefly of sodium thiosulfate; used for fixing.

ISO rating — Classification of film emulsion relating to its sensitivity to light.

Light meter — Instrument used to measure light reflected from or falling on a subject.

Macrophotography — Close-up photography; the photographic rendition is larger than the object.

Negative — Developed film that shows the image in reverse tones of the original subject.

Print — Positive rendition of a subject usually made from a negative.

Refraction — Bending of light rays when they pass from one medium to another.

Stop Bath — Weak acetic acid solution used to stop development of film or paper.

Report

1. Define refraction.

2. How does a camera form an image?

3. What is the primary difference between ISO 50 and ISO 200 films?

4. Why is oblique illumination so useful in forensic photography?

5. Assume you used a film with a 50 ISO value to photograph an object while your camera was set to an f-stop of 5.6 and an exposure time of 1 second. Even though the camera was sharply focused, the resulting image was somewhat blurry. How could you improve the image of the object?

6. Develop your photographs based on the techniques in Experiment 16 and use them to prepare a display.

16

Basic Black-and-White Photography

Purpose

Learn the basic procedures of developing negatives and preparing black-and-white photographic enlargements of negatives.

Equipment and Supplies

1. Negative developing solutions and equipment for 35-mm film
2. Photographic paper, developing solutions, and trays
3. Dark room with sinks, running water, safelights, and counter space
4. 33-mm enlarger
5. Thermometer
6. Magnifying glass
7. Ruler or appropriate scale
8. Enlarger timer

Procedure

When film is exposed to light, the silver compounds embedded in the film emulsion undergo a chemical reaction and produce a hidden image that can be made visible by application of developing chemicals. A negative developer reacts with the emulsion and removes the unaffected silver halides. A stop bath halts the developer action, and a fixing compound sets the silver image of the subject onto the film.

Figure 16.1 shows the equipment necessary to develop black-and-white prints. Figure 16.2 shows dark room components: (1) developer tray, (2) stop bath tray, (3) fixing solution tray, (4) washing tray, (5) squeegee table, and (6) drum-type print drier.

Film Development

1. In the darkroom, open the camera and remove the film exposed during Experiment 15.
2. Place the strip of 35-mm film onto a film reel; place the reel into a canister.
3. After securing the canister, turn on the room lights.
4. Pour the appropriate developer into the canister. The developing chemicals should be kept at room temperature and premixed according to the manufacturer's instructions. Allow the film to develop for 3 to 5 minutes.
5. Pour out the developer into a collection container and rinse the film with water.
6. Pour out the water rinse, and add stop bath to the canister. Wait 30 seconds, pour out the stop bath, and rinse the film with water.
7. Discard the water rinse, and add fixing solution to the canister. Fix the film for 10 minutes.
8. Remove the film from the canister and wash with water for 30 minutes.
9. Squeegee the film surface before drying.

Enlargement of Negatives (Figure 16.1)

1. Place the dried 35-mm negative strip into the negative carrier of the enlarger.
2. Place the negative carrier into the enlarger.
3. The emulsion side of the negative must face downward, toward the enlargement easel.
4. Turn the room lights out; work only with safelights.
5. Place a sheet of old print paper into an easel board to aid the viewing, focusing, and sizing of the image.
6. Turn the enlarger on, and open the lens to its widest aperture.
7. To produce the desired photographic print, move the enlarger unit up or down to achieve the proper size image. Use a scale to size the image.
8. Move the bellows up or down to properly focus the image.
9. Set the aperture stop to f-8 and the exposure time to 1 second.
10. Turn the enlarger off and replace the old print paper with a sheet of unexposed photographic paper in the easel.
11. Expose the paper and develop according to the procedure below.

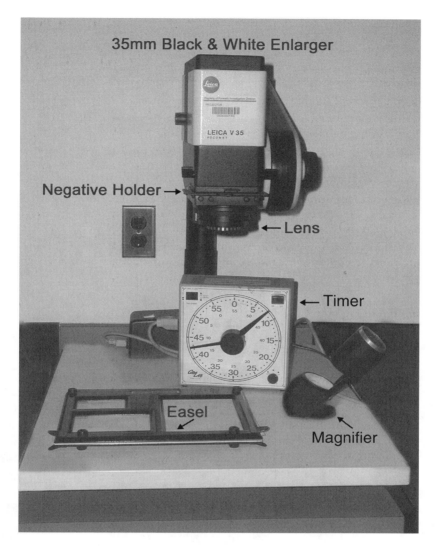

FIGURE 16.1
Equipment necessary for developing black-and-white photographic prints.

Print Development (Figure 16.2)

1. Place the exposed paper into the developer. The developing chemicals should be kept at room temperature and premixed according to the manufacturer's instructions. The image should form and be completely developed in 1 to 2 minutes.

2. Wash the print and immerse in the stop bath for 5 seconds.

3. Wash the print and immerse in the fix for 10 minutes.

4. Remove the print from the fix and wash it in running water for 30 minutes.

5. Squeegee the surface; drain and dry the print with a drying drum.

6. Adjust the aperture, exposure, and filter of the enlarger until results are optimum.

FIGURE 16.2
Darkroom photographic printing equipment and solutions: (1) developer tray, (2) stopbath tray, (3) fixing solution tray, (4) washing tray, (5) squeegee table, (6) drum-type print drier.

Report

1. Critique the quality of your photographs.

2. Prepare a court display of your evidence photographs as directed by your instructor.

3. Hand in your court display at the start of the next laboratory session or as otherwise instructed by your professor.

17

Collection of Footwear Evidence

Purpose

Learn the basic techniques of recovering footwear evidence from crime scenes; learn the jargon of footwear examination and gain added knowledge of the concepts of identity and individualization.

Footwear evidence is a material surface that retains and portrays undersole and heel patterns and reveals wear patterns and individualizing characteristics. Footwear images are acquired by residue transfer or compression of loose material by the undersole of a shoe, boot, or other footwear. Footwear evidence can be presented as two- or three-dimensional prints. Laboratory shoe print examinations have one or more of the following objectives:

1. Obtaining investigative information about questioned footwear impressions (type of footwear, manufacturer, model, general type).
2. Comparing questioned impressions with known footwear impressions to include or exclude suspects.
3. Associating people with places such as crime scenes.
4. Reconstructing crimes.

Equipment and Supplies

1. Questioned two-dimensional footwear residue prints and three-dimensional impressions provided by your instructor
2. Supplies necessary to document footwear evidence
   - 35-mm camera
   - Film
   - Photographic accessories (i.e., tripod, level)
   - Lighting or illumination sources (ultraviolet, infrared)

3. Supplies necessary to collect two- and three-dimensional footwear evidence
    - Clear lifters (11 × 14 in. and 8 × 10 in.)
    - Gel lifters (black, white, and clear)
    - Electrostatic dust lifting device kit — includes roller, tray, lifting foil, alligator clips, ruler, charging unit, and instructions
    - Casting materials (dental stone, silicon)
    - Plastic ziplock bags
    - Plastic bottles filled with water
4. Magnifying glass
5. Various light sources

Procedure

1. Locate the questioned footwear print. If you are at a crime scene, employ the appropriate searching procedures to locate the print.
2. If a two-dimensional residue print is the goal, use the oblique lighting technique to locate latent footwear prints. Figure 17.1 shows a photographic set-up for revealing a latent footwear print. The set-up consists of oblique lighting, a level, a 35-mm camera on a tripod, and high contrast black-and-white film. A digital camera can be used. Fill the frame with the image and always use a scale.
3. Document the footwear print by photographing it.
4. If you are working with a dust print, first document it photographically, then lift it with a clear plastic adhesive lifter. Figure 17.2 shows the procedure.
5. If available and appropriate, use an electrostatic dust lifting device to lift the dust footwear print (Figure 17.3). The procedure is as follows :
    A. If the print is on a movable object such as a newspaper, place the newspaper on a metal tray. If the print is not on a movable surface, electrically ground the area immediately around the print.
    B. Place the dark side of the foil on top of the newspaper or other object containing the print; apply the electrodes.
    C. Apply an electrical charge to the foil by engaging the power supply switch.
    D. Press down with a roller; move the roller back and forth until the foil is flat.
    E. Turn the foil over to reveal the print.
    F. Review electrostatic dust lifting device instructions.
6. If a three-dimensional impression is found, use the oblique lighting technique to photograph the impression.
7. Cast the impression using the technique shown in Figure 17.4. The general rules are as follows:
    A. Shallow impressions in sand or soil less than 1 in. deep should be cast with dental stone or silicone (Figure 17.5). Dental stone is a specially formulated casting plaster. It can be mixed in a plastic bag (2 lb dental stone and 12 oz water) and does not require reinforcement.

B. Deep impressions should be cast with dental stone.

C. Impressions in snow and ice can be cast with paraffin (snow wax) or sulfur.

D. To cast a footwear impression in soil, remove loose objects and spray the print with clear lacquer. Figure 17.5 depicts a finished dental stone cast that includes fine details.

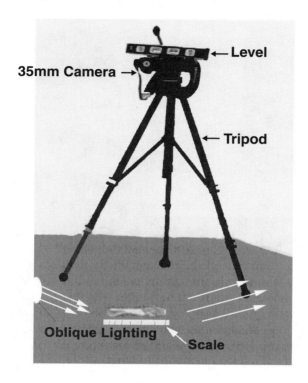

FIGURE 17.1

The photographic set-up for documenting a latent, residue footwear print using oblique lighting, a level, and 35-mm camera on a tripod with high contrast black-and-white film. A digital camera can be employed. Remember to fill the frame with the image of the print, and always use a scale.

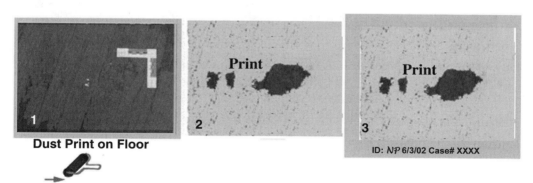

1. **Place clear lifter over print and press down with roller.**

2. **Remove clear print lifter.**

3. **Place lift on a sheet of contasting glossy paper.**

FIGURE 17.2

The procedure for lifting a residue dust print with a clear plastic lifter.

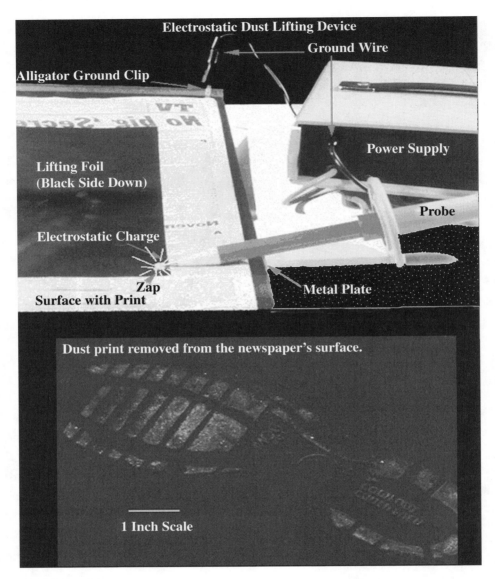

FIGURE 17.3
Electrostatic dust lifting device is used to lift dust prints off all types of surfaces.

1.

Impressive in Soil

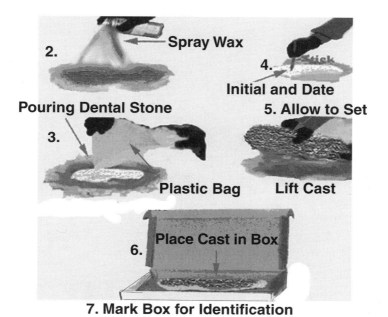

2. ← **Spray Wax**

Pouring Dental Stone

4. **Stick**

Initial and Date

5. Allow to Set

3.

Plastic Bag   **Lift Cast**

Place Cast in Box

6.

7. Mark Box for Identification

FIGURE 17.4
Casting a three-dimensional footwear print.

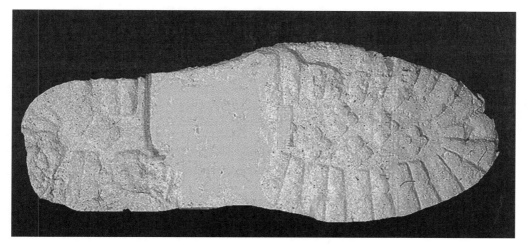

FIGURE 17.5
Finished dental stone cast of footwear impression.

Report

1. Record all observations (i.e., time, date, location; condition of the crime scene and evidence; location of the evidence).

2. Draw a rough sketch of the footwear evidence and the crime scene.

3. As a homework assignment, use your rough sketch, lifts or casts, notes, and photographs to prepare a detailed scale drawing. Refer to Experiment 8 to determine the elements that should be included.

4. Hand in your drawing with all exemplars at the start of your next laboratory session or as otherwise directed by your instructor.

Identification and Matching of Footwear Evidence

Purpose

Learn the concepts, rationale, and procedures for identifying and comparing footwear evidence from crime scenes; learn to prepare court displays.

Equipment and Supplies

1. Examples of standard footwear
2. Squeegee
3. Adhesive clear lifter tape or Kodak roller transport film
4. Water
5. Questioned footwear exemplars from a crime scene
6. Magnifying glass
7. Photographic mounting board

Procedure

Footwear impression evidence can:

1. Help identify or eliminate a suspect
2. Determine the brand of a shoe by comparison wth a database
3. Determine size
4. Positively identify a shoe by its unique characteristics

5. Prove an individual's presence at a crime scene
6. Aid in reconstructing a crime scene
7. Show the number of perpetrators involved
8. Help prove involvement in a crime
9. Reveal the time frame when the impression was made
10. Reveal a sequence of events
11. Prove or disprove an alibi

Preparation of Known Standards

1. Moisten the outsole of a known item of footwear with water. Figure 18.1 shows known and standard footwear.
2. Tap off excess water; remove remaining water with a dry cloth.
3. Apply fingerprint powder to the outsole with a fiberglass brush. Three or more applications may be required.
4. Place a piece of clear adhesive lifter or a moistened piece of roll transport film adhesive side up onto a cushioning pad.
5. Put a protective sock or plastic bag on your foot and place your foot into the known footwear.
6. Attempt to walk normally and step onto the film.
7. Place the film on a table and allow it to air dry. A hair dyer can accelerate drying. If adhesive lifter is used, cover it with clear plastic sheet and press down with a roller (see Experiment 17).

Questioned Print Examination

A questioned footwear examination establishes class characteristics (pattern, size length), determines wear areas and patterns, and reveals individualizing or accidental characteristics. Figure 18.2 shows class, wear, individualizing characteristics, and patterns.

Typical features to be observed include class characteristics produced during manufacture (design of sole), wear patterns (WP) produced during normal wear (i.e., worn-down heel areas), and accidental or individualizing marks or patterns (AP) produced by random chance during normal wear.

Accidental or identifying characteristics are cuts, tears, gouges, adherence of foreign bodies (gum, pebbles, fragments of glass), and wear marks that randomly appear when a shoe is worn. These characteristics can often individualize a known shoe to a questioned print.

Class characteristics are intentional or unavoidable characteristics that repeat during manufacture and appear on all shoes. The characteristics are size, shape, pattern design, and manufacturing characteristics.

Wear patterns are the result of random removal of material from the outer sole and heel as shoes are worn. Wear patterns serve as supplemental identifying features. Most people usually wear their shoes out in same manner. As a result, wear patterns can help associate questioned footwear prints to known pieces of footwear.

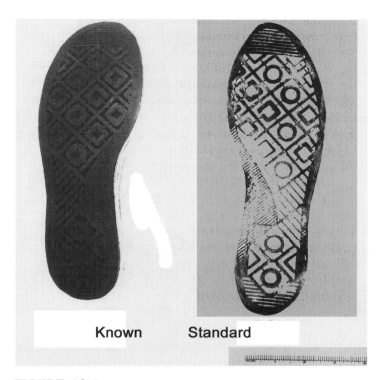

FIGURE 18.1

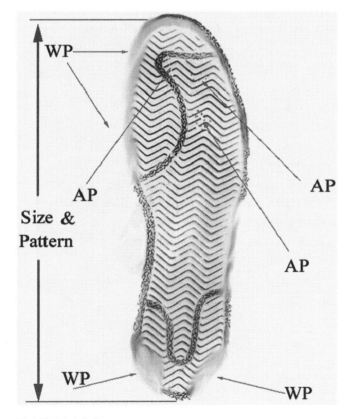

FIGURE 18.2

Evaluation

Always compare the class, wear, and accidental features of the questioned impression to the known one. Do not compare the known to the questioned. Since identifying characteristics change as footwear is worn, it is likely that certain characteristics will not be found in both the questioned and known impressions. Depending on depth and location, an identifying characteristic can be eliminated in 1 to 14 days of continuous wear. Shapes and sizes of characteristics can also vary over time.

Conclusions

1. For a positive identification, **all** class characteristics of the questioned impression must be seen in the known impression; one or more identifying characteristics must appear on both questioned and known impressions.
2. In a positive elimination, known footwear will not possess the same class features as questioned prints.
3. *Not suitable for comparison* means not enough of the questioned print is available for examination.
4. Consistent in class characteristics (same pattern, size, length, width).
5. Consistent in class characteristics and wear pattern.

Footwear Glossary

Heel — A footwear component attached to the rear part of the outsole.

Heel area — Rear portion of the outsole.

Logo — Name, design, or pattern that appears on the sides or outsoles of athletic shoes; trademark of the manufacturer.

Midsole — Component placed between the outsole and the shoe upper; not found on all shoes.

Outsole — Bottom part of a shoe that makes contact with the ground.

Shoe upper — Part of a shoe excluding the outsole and midsole.

Toe bumper guard — Thick strip of rubber placed across the top of the toe box or the vamp to increase strength and durability.

Tongue — Tongue-shaped strip of material lying beneath the shoelaces and covering the instep of the foot.

Report

1. Report your findings after examination of a questioned footwear print.

2. Justify your conclusions.

3. List the matching features of the questioned and known footwear prints.

4. Prepare court displays. Figure 18.3 shows a residue print prepared for use in court. Figure 18.4 shows a class match comparison.

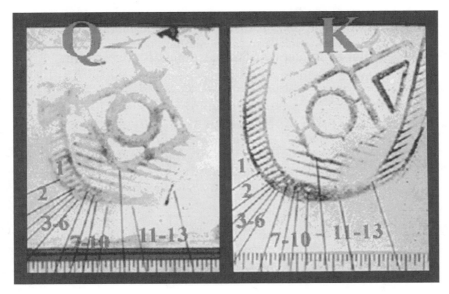

FIGURE 18.3

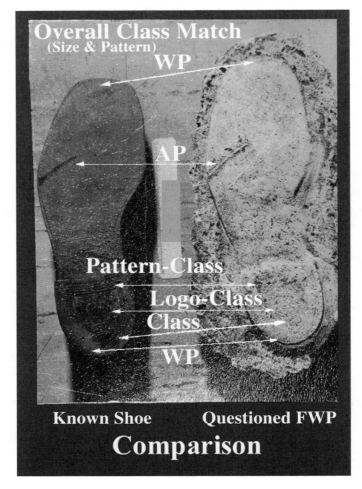

FIGURE 18.4

Tool Mark Examination

Purpose

Learn the concepts, rationales, and procedures of recognizing, documenting, collecting, and comparing tool mark evidence.

A tool mark is an impression, gouge, gash, slash, groove, channel, dent, indentation, hole, scrape, graze, abrasion, scratch, cut, or striation made on an object or person by the application of a tool. It is important to note that a tool for forensic purposes is defined as a device or implement that can produce the questioned marks.

Equipment and Supplies

1. Questioned tool marks on items provided by your instructor
2. Questioned tools provided by your instructor
3. Photographic equipment
4. Film
5. Magnifying glass
6. Stereomicroscope
7. Materials for making standard (known) tool marks
   - Tool (screwdriver, hammer, saw, etc.)
   - Material on which to place tool marks made by the above tool (i.e., wood, lead sheets, aluminum sheets, copper sheets, etc.)
8. Casting silicone
9. Spatula
10. Scale or ruler

Procedure

Tool mark evidence can:

1. Help identify or eliminate a suspect.
2. Determine a general or specific type tool and size.
3. Positively identify a tool by its unique characteristics.
4. Prove an individual's presence at a crime scene.
5. Aid in reconstructing a crime scene.
6. Help prove involvement in a crime.
7. Prove or disprove an alibi.

Questioned Tool Mark Examination

1. Examine the item you receive for obvious tool marks and foreign or unusual marks.
2. Document and photograph the questioned marks. Figure 19.1 shows suspected tool marks on a mortise lock.
3. Examine the questioned marks *in situ* under oblique lighting.
4. Prepare casting silicone according to the manufacturer's instruction (Figure 19.2).
5. Apply casting silicone to the questioned marks (Figure 19.3).
6. Allow the silicone to set about 15 minutes and photograph it.
7. Remove the silicone cast for examination (Figure 19.4) and comparison with known tools.

Preliminary Examination of Questioned Tool Marks

1. If possible, establish the questioned tool mark's class characteristics: pattern, size, length, type of tool.
2. Determine the questioned tool mark's wear areas and overall wear patterns.
3. Examine it for individualizing or accidental characteristics.

Preparation of Known Standards

1. Remove all trace evidence from the surface of the suspected tool.
2. Make several tool marks on a soft metal surface (copper or alumium sheet) with the suspected tool (Figure 19.5). A softer metal is used to prevent alteration of the tool.
3. Attempt to simulate the manner in which the questioned tool marks were made. Try to use the same angle, degree of pressure, stroke, etc.
4. Cast the known tool marks with silicone (Figure 19.3).

FIGURE 19.1
Photograph of possible tool marks on a mortise lock.

FIGURE 19.2
Mix the casting silicone as needed with a spatula.

FIGURE 19.3
Application of casting silicone onto suspected tool marks.

FIGURE 19.4
Gently remove the silicone cast for further examination.

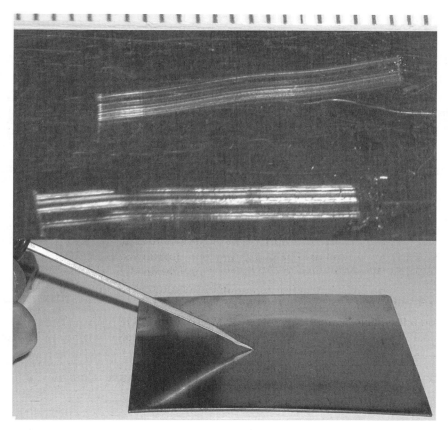

FIGURE 19.5
Known tool marks being made with suspected tool.

Examination and Comparison of Questioned and Known Tool Marks

1. **Typical features** to be observed during a tool mark examination and comparison: class characteristics produced during manufacturing of the tool, including design, size, model, accidental or individualizing marks produced randomly during routine use.

2. **Class characteristics** are intentional or unavoidable characteristics that repeat during manufacture; they are components of all tools of their type produced and include shape, pattern design, manufacturing characteristics, and wear caused by machinery.

3. **Accidental or identifying characteristics** are cuts, tears, gouges, and other marks that appear randomly when a tool is used. These are often used to individualize a known tool to questioned tool marks.

4. Compare the questioned and known silicones cast under the stereomicroscope. Make all necessary measurements. If possible, compare the known marks on the metal surface with the questioned marks on the questioned metal surface.

Evaluation

Always compare the questioned impression to the known. Do not compare the known to the questioned. Compare the class and accidental features of the questioned to the known. Since identifying characteristics are constantly formed and lost by virtue of use of a tool, it is likely that the same characteristics will not be found on both the questioned and known impressions. Depending on the depth and location, an identifying characteristic can be eliminated in 1 to 14 days of continuous use. Shapes and sizes of characteristics can also vary over time.

Conclusions

1. For a positive identification, all class characteristics of the questioned impression must be present in the known; one or more identifying characteristics must appear on both questioned and known marks.

2. In a positive elimination, a known tool does not possess the same class features as the questioned tool marks.

3. *Not suitable for comparison* means the questioned mark is not sufficient for examination.

4. Consistent in class characteristics — the known marks made by the standard tool have the same general features as the questioned marks, i.e., size, shape, design, etc.

Report

1. Report your findings after examination of questioned tool marks.

2. Justify your conclusions.

3. List the matching features of the questioned and known tool marks.

Experiment 20

Glass Fractures and Direction of Force

Purpose

Learn the concepts, rationale, and procedures necessary to determine the direction from which force that breaks window glass was applied.

Equipment and Supplies

1. Questioned pieces of broken window glass and plexiglass provided by your instructor
2. Thick leather gloves for handling the glass and plexiglass (broken glass and plexiglass are extremely sharp; you **must** wear protective leather gloves when you handle such evidence)
3. Magnifying glass
4. Stereomicroscope

Procedure

When sufficient force is applied to glass, various types of fracture lines appear. The lines usually form a structure that looks like an insect web. The two distinct classes of fracture lines are radial and concentric lines. Figure 20.1 illustrates both types of lines. The general rule for radial fractures is *right, rear, radial*. That means the force was applied to the opposite or rear side of the glass where the conchoidal fracture lines form a right angle to the surface (see Figure 20.1). A projectile that strikes the surface of a piece of glass or plastic at a right or 90° angle will produce a cone-shaped hole. The peak of the cone-shaped hole is the point of impact.

1. Review all your notes and readings concerning glass examination.
2. Listen intently to and heed the instructions for safe handling of sharp objects.
3. Place the leather safety gloves on both hands before you handle the glass.
4. Note the side of the questioned glass that is most soiled.
5. Examine the questioned item for radial and concentric fractures.
6. Use the stereomicroscope to examine the broken edges of radial fractures for feather-shaped stress marks known as conchoidal fractures.

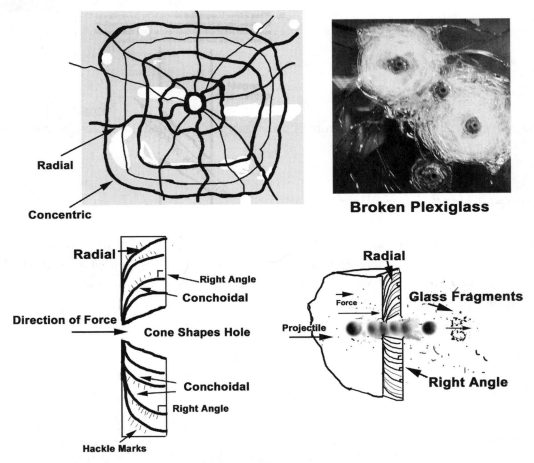

FIGURE 20.1
Depiction of various fractures in glass.

Report

1. Report your findings.

2. Justify your conclusions.

3. Make a sketch of the fracture.

4. Why do you think you were told to note the most soiled side of the window pane?

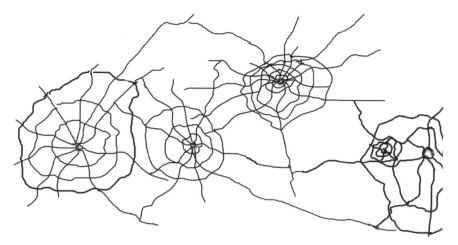

FIGURE 20.2
A sequence of five bullet holes fired into a pane of glass.

5. Figure 20.2 shows a sequence of five bullet holes fired into a pane of glass. Is this sequence possible? If not, explain why. If yes, explain why. What, if anything, is wrong with this sequence? Explain. Which fracture came first; which came last. Explain.

21

Thin Layer Chromatography: Separation of Dyes in Ballpoint Inks

Purpose

This exercise will demonstrate a powerful technique that allows chemists and forensic scientists to separate the components of a mixture. The general name for the technique is *chromatography* (separation of colors). Many types of chromatography are available including gas–liquid, gas–solid, liquid–solid, and high performance (pressure) liquid. All the types are based on different levels of attraction of the materials to be separated for the stationary and mobile phases.

Thin layer chromatography (TLC) is one of the most common forms of liquid–solid chromatography. A thin layer of an active absorbent is bound onto a glass plate. The sample dissolved in a solvent is spotted onto the plate near one edge. An appropriate solvent is placed in a chamber and allowed to equilibrate. The plate is placed in the chamber. The solvent travels up the plate by capillary action. Different materials (e.g., the dyes in ballpoint pen ink) are separated on the plate depending on certain chemical or physical characteristics. The distance migrated by the dye when divided by the total distance traveled by the solvent from the spotting point is referred as the R_f of that compound and is consistent for that chromatography system and characteristic for the compound of interest. Figure 21.1 illustrates the equipment necessary for TLC of inks.

Many materials of interest are not colored and are invisible under normal light, i.e., room light. In such cases, ultraviolet light can be used to locate these materials. The plate containing the test materials is observed under ultraviolet illumination. The areas of the plate that exhibit fluorescing spots should be circled with a pencil.

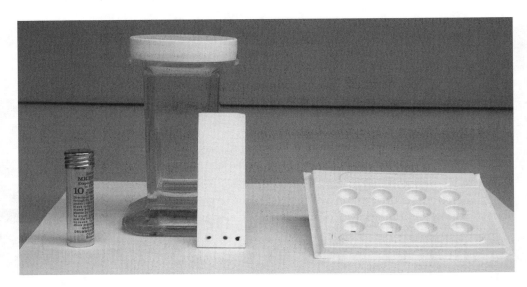

FIGURE 21.1
Equipment necessary to do thin layer chromatography of inks.

Equipment and Supplies

1. TLC plates
2. Silica Gel G, 250 μ thick, 1 × 3 inches
3. TLC development tanks (Coplin jars with covers)
4. Glass spotting pipettes, 5 and 10 μ
5. Porcelain spot plates
6. Ruler
7. Sharp pencil
8. Solvents: acetone, water, ethanol, methyl alcohol, 2-propyl alcohol, n-butanol, ethyl acetate, reagent grade pyridine (All organic reagents should be used under a ventilation hood)
9. Blotter paper to hasten chamber equilibration
10. Ultraviolet light (UV)

Procedure

1. Obtain samples of known inks and an unknown from your instructor.
2. Mix acetone, ethanol, and water to the TLC tank in a ratio of 14:7:6. Add blotter, then cover and mix well; allow to equilibrate for 30 minutes.
3. Mix 10 mL of extraction solvent (acetone, methyl alcohol, and water in a ratio of 4:5:1).

4. Place a small sample of each standard and the unknown into separate wells on the spot plate. Add a few drops of extraction solvent. Mix well with a glass rod or metal paper clip. If the ink does not dissolve, try a mixture of pyridine and water (9:1 ratio) or warm pyridine. Evaporate to a small volume. **Use all organic reagents under a ventilation hood.**

5. Draw a very light pencil line across the bottom of the plate, about 5 mm from the edge.

6. Using the pipettes, spot 5 aliquots of this solvent onto the plate at the x, employing a gentle stream of exhaled air to keep the spot small. Repeat as necessary to obtain a strong spot. Do not overspot. Allow the plate to dry.

7. Make sure the solvent does not extend over the spotting line. Place the plate into the tank and cover. Allow the plate to develop (solvent will migrate up the plate) to 50 mm past the location of the original spot. Remove the plate and allow it to dry.

8. Calculate the R_f for each spot in each ink standard and the unknown.

9. If the dyes do not separate well, try n-butanol, 2-propyl alcohol, and distilled water in a 2:1:1 ratio as a development solvent.

10. Compare the results and determine which known matches your unknown.

Report

1. Figure 21.2 shows a TLC comparison of three black inks. Calculate the R_f for each of the spots.

2. Identify your unknown.

3. Write a short description of what you learned in this exercise.

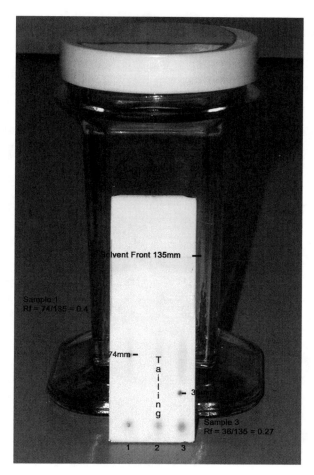

FIGURE 21.2
Comparison of three black inks with TLC.

Experiment 22

Bloodstain Pattern Geometry (Part A)

Purpose

Acquire familiarity with the basic geometric shapes and patterns formed by droplets of blood when they impact various target surfaces and learn the basic concepts and rationales used to recognize, document, and interpret bloodstain evidence.

Equipment and Supplies

1. Artificial blood (see instructions for preparation below)
2. 30- to 60-mL dropper bottle or 50-mL beaker for storing artificial blood
3. Disposable pipettes
4. Plain white typing paper
5. 12-in. square pieces of cardboard
6. 12-in. square pieces of 1/8-in.-thick, smooth, clear or white sheets of acrylic
7. 12-in. square pieces of plywood
8. Paper towels
9. Tape measure
10. Ruler
11. Meter stick
12. Protractor

Procedure

1. Draw a quantity of artificial blood into a pipette or dropper bottle and wipe off any excess from the outside of the tip with a paper towel. Be careful not to include air bubbles in the liquid.

2. Drop a single drop of artificial blood straight down onto each surface texture to be tested from heights of 1 in., 2 in., 36 in., and 72 in. Figure 22.1 shows patterns formed when a drop of artificial blood is dropped onto a piece of white typing paper from various heights.

3. The test materials should be placed flat on the floor and the pipette should be held perpendicular to the surfaces when the drops are released.

4. Make your observations while the stains are wet and after the stains are thoroughly dried.

Bloodstain Pattern Glossary

Angle of impact — Angle at which a blood drop strikes a target surface.

Back spatter — Blood that travels back toward the direction of the initiating force.

Blood spatter — Pattern formed when blood touches a surface.

Cast-off blood — Blood collected by and then cast from a moving object.

Contact stain — Result of contact of a bloody article and a surface.

Point of origin — Location from which blood originates.

Smear — Pattern left when a bloody object is wiped across a surface.

Target — Surface on which blood is deposited.

Transfer pattern — Pattern transferred to a surface when a bloody object comes into contact with it.

Artificial Blood Preparations

1. Mix 4 oz of evaporated milk, 2 to 3 tbsp of tomato paste, and red food dye to the viscosity of blood. Use water as a solvent. The mixture should be freshly made. It can be stored in a refrigerator for a few days.

2. Mix Carnation® dry milk, red food dye, and water to the viscosity of blood.

3. Mix white corn syrup and red food dye until the mixture has the appearance of blood.

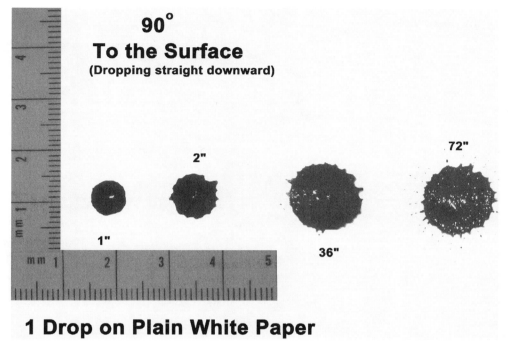

1 Drop on Plain White Paper

FIGURE 22.1

Patterns that are formed when one drop of artificial blood is dropped straight down onto a piece of white typing paper from various heights.

Report

1. Report your observations.

2. Sketch or photograph each specimen. (See Figure 22.1.)

3. For each surface texture examined, make the following observations:

   A. Describe the texture of the surface: hard or soft; smooth or rough; porous or nonporous; absorbent or nonabsorbent.

   B. Describe the edge characteristics of the resulting stains.

   C. Measure the diameter (in mm) of each drop.

   D. Describe the extent of peripheral satellite spattering.

   E. Discuss what effect the changing drop heights had on the resulting stains.

   F. Experiment with other surface textures such as floor tiles, carpets, textiles.

Experiment 23

Bloodstain Pattern Geometry (Part B)

Purpose

Acquire familiarity with the basic geometric shapes and patterns formed by droplets of blood when they impact different target surfaces at 45, 60, and 70° angles. Experiment with smears and contact pattern transfers. Learn the effects of various impact angles on the geometry of blood droplets and the concepts and rationales that are used in the study, and to interpret complex bloodstain patterns.

Equipment and Supplies

1. Artificial blood prepared in accordance with instructions in Experiment 22
2. 30- to 60-mL dropper bottle or 50-mL beaker
3. Disposable pipettes
4. Plain white typing paper
5. 12-in. square pieces of cardboard
6. 12-in. square pieces of 1/8-in.-thick, smooth, clear or white sheets of acrylic
7. 12-in. square pieces of plywood
8. Paper towels
9. Tape measure
10. Ruler
11. Meter stick
12. Protractor

Procedure

1. Draw artificial blood into the pipette or dropper and wipe off any excess from the outside of the tip with a paper towel. Be careful not to include any air bubbles with the blood drops.

2. The test surfaces should be placed at various angles to the floor. Hold the loaded pipette or dropper perpendicular to the floor and release the blood. Figure 23.1 shows the technique.

3. Release a single drop of artificial blood straight downward onto each surface texture to be tested from a height of 12 in. at impact angles of 45, 60, and 70° (Figure 23.2 shows appearances of droplets after impact). Prepare one test surface for a drop of artificial blood impacting a surface at 60° from a height of 24 in. (see Figure 23.3).

4. Make your observations while the stains are wet and after the stains are thoroughly dried.

5. Repeat the experiment on several different surfaces.

6. Prepare one smear and one contact pattern on separate pieces of plain white paper (see Figure 23.4).

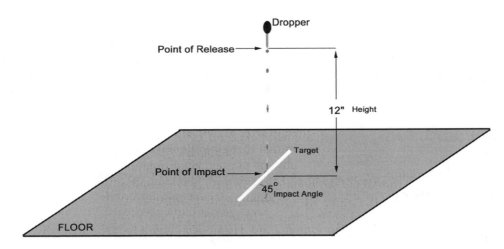

FIGURE 23.1
The application of the test droplets of artificial blood.

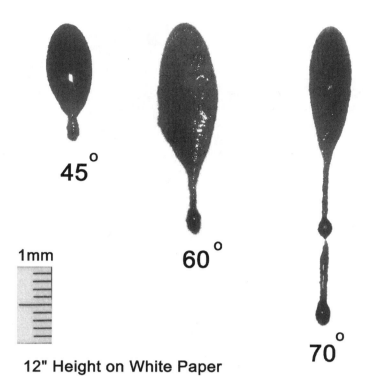

FIGURE 23.2
Appearance of blood droplets after impacting a plain white paper surface at various angles from a height of 12 in.

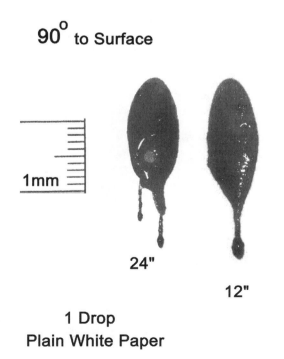

FIGURE 23.3
The appearance of two blood droplets after impacting a piece of plain white paper 60° from a height of 24 in. and 12 in.

155

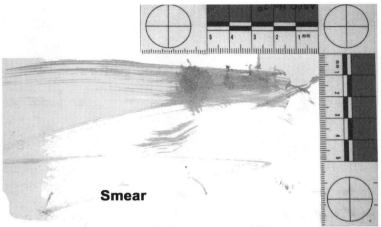

Smear

Contact Transfer of Pattern

FIGURE 23.4

Report

1. Report your observations.

2. Sketch or photograph each specimen. (See Figures 23.2 and 23.3.)

3. For each surface texture examined, make the following observations:

A. Describe the texture of the surface: hard of soft; smooth or rough; porous or nonporous; absorbent or nonabsorbent.

B. Describe the edge characteristics of the resulting stains.

C. Measure the diameter and length (in mm) of each pattern.

D. Describe the extent of peripheral satellite spattering.

E. Discuss what effect the changing drop heights had on the resulting stains.

F. Experiment with other surface textures such as floor tiles, carpets, textiles.

G. How do the 12-in. and 24-in. 60° impact angle test patterns differ on plain white paper?

H. How do the smear and contact transfer patterns differ?

Experiment 24

Forgery Detection

Purpose

Introduce the basic concepts and rationales necessary to recognize, document, identify, and compare a handwritten forgery.

Equipment and Supplies

1. Known handwriting (script) exemplars (prepared on index cards and in tables, see pages 162 and 163)
2. Known printed handwriting exemplars (prepared on index cards and in tables, see pages 162 and 163)
3. Questioned documents prepared by students (prepared on index cards and in tables, see pages 162 and 163)
4. Hand magnifying glass
5. Stereomicroscope
6. Scale
7. Ruler
8. Protractor
9. Blue pen (same type must be used by all students)
10. 35-mm camera
11. Black-and-white film
12. 3-in. by 5-in. white index cards

Procedure

Most casework performed by forensic document examiners involves identifying the authorship of handwritten documents, such as historical records, letters, wills, and checks. The primary technique is the comparison of the handwriting of a known author or suspected forger with the handwriting on a questioned document. The four basic methods used by forgers to carry out their work are tracing, freehand copying, mechanical lifting, and optical and/or printing reproduction.

This experiment relates to the use and detection of handwritten forgeries. It requires preparation of documents by the students before they proceed with the comparison and identification aspects of the experiment.

1. Preparation of documents. Your instructor will direct you to prepare certain handwriting exemplars and documents. Follow all instructions precisely. Do not add any identifying information to the examplars.

   A. **Preparation of Script Handwriting Exemplar (Normal):** In your normal handwriting, write the following five items on separate index cards:

      1. Four score and seven years ago, our fathers brought forth on this continent a new nation, conceived in liberty and dedicated to the proposition that all men are created equal.

      2. The little sly, quick, clever, young, red fox jumped over the big, drowsy, lazy, guard dog.

      3. Goodnight, goodnight! Parting is such sweet sorrow; shall I say goodnight, 'til it be morrow?

      4. 1111, 2222, 3333, 4444, 5555, 6666, 7777, 8888, 9999, 0000

      5. - - ,, // !! ?? () "" <> ## $$ %% && ++ [].. ;; ::

   B. **Preparation of Script Handwriting Exemplar (Disguised):** Disguise your normal handwriting and write the five items below on separate index cards:

      1. Four score and seven years ago, our fathers brought forth on this continent a new nation, conceived in liberty and dedicated to the proposition that all men are created equal.

      2. The little sly, quick, clever, young, red fox jumped over the big, drowsy, lazy, guard dog.

      3. Goodnight, goodnight! Parting is such sweet sorrow; shall I say goodnight, 'til it be morrow?

      4. 1111, 2222, 3333, 4444, 5555, 6666, 7777, 8888, 9999, 0000

      5. - - ,, // !! ?? () "" <> ## $$ %% && ++ [].. ;; ::

   C. **Preparation of Printed Handwriting Exemplar (Normal):** Using your normal hand, print the following five items on index cards:

      1. Four score and seven years ago, our fathers brought forth on this continent a new nation, conceived in liberty and dedicated to the proposition that all men are created equal.

      2. The little sly, quick, clever, young, red fox jumped over the big, drowsy, lazy, guard dog.

      3. Goodnight, goodnight! Parting is such sweet sorrow; shall I say goodnight, 'til it be morrow?

      4. 1111, 2222, 3333, 4444, 5555, 6666, 7777, 8888, 9999, 0000

      5. - - ,, // !! ?? () "" <> ## $$ %% && ++ [].. ;; ::

D. **Preparation of Printed Handwriting Exemplar (Disguised):** Disguising your normal hand, print the following five items on index cards:

1. Four score and seven years ago, our fathers brought forth on this continent a new nation, conceived in liberty and dedicated to the proposition that all men are created equal.

2. The little sly, quick, clever, young, red fox jumped over the big, drowsy, lazy, guard dog.

3. Goodnight, goodnight! Parting is such sweet sorrow; shall I say goodnight, 'til it be morrow?

4. 1111, 2222, 3333, 4444, 5555, 6666, 7777, 8888, 9999, 0000

5. - - „ // !! ?? () ”” <> ## $$ %% && ++ [].. ;; ::

E. **Preparation of Questioned Exemplars:** In the empty spaces of Table 24.1, sign the name as Joseph John Doe. Write in your normal freehand style as if you were signing an important document. Use the empty spaces in Table 24.2 to practice copying Joseph John Doe as you wrote it in Table 24.1.

TABLE 24.1
Model Signature Exemplars

Joseph John Doe	

TABLE 24.2
Copies of Signatures from Table 24.1

Joseph John Doe	

F. **Preparation of Questioned Check:** Using Figure 24.1, prepare a check to cash for $1000.00. Sign it as Joseph John Doe. Endorse (also as Joseph John Doe) the reverse side of the check that appears in the figure and add your account number 20222 2842 to your endorsement.

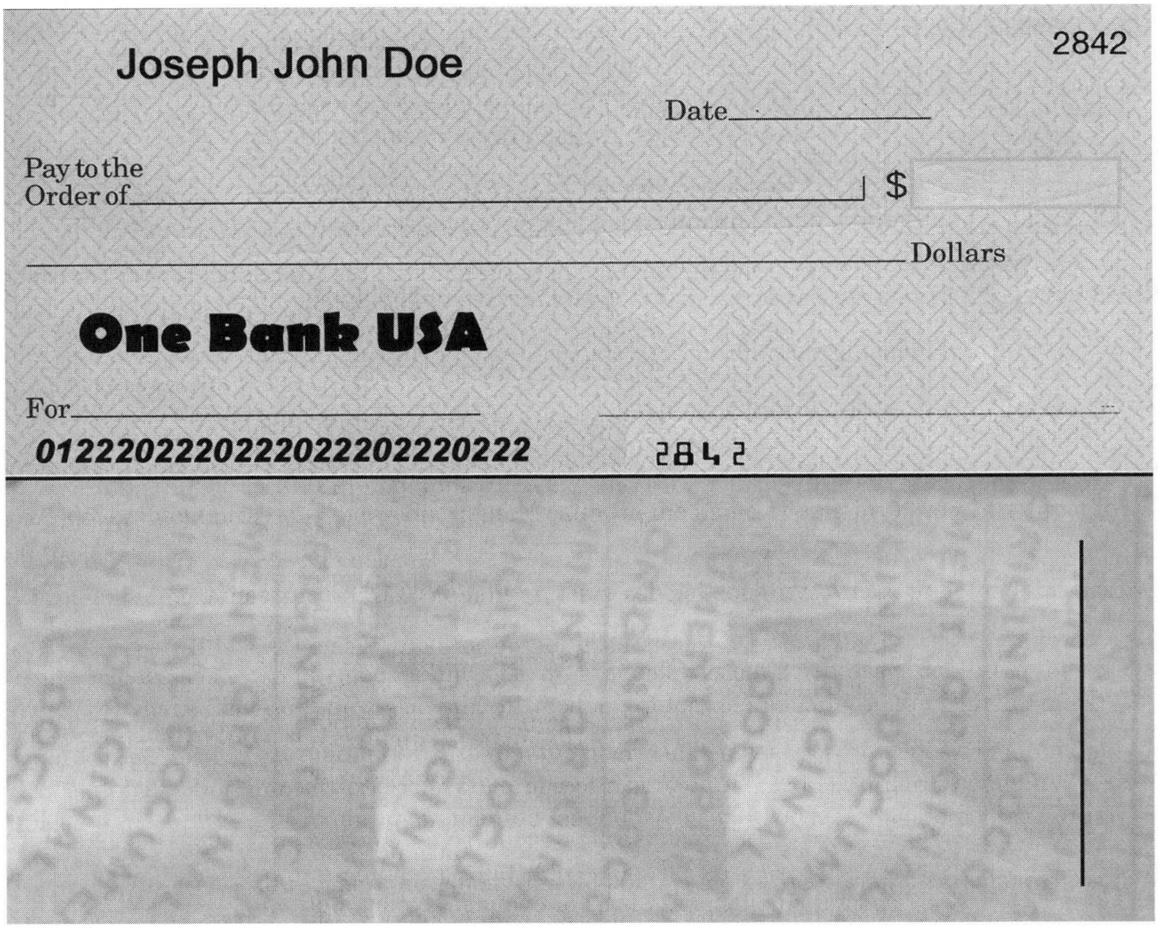

FIGURE 24.1
Blank check.

2. Write your name on one of the index cards provided by your instructor. Return it to the instructor along with the exemplars you prepared. The instructor will store the materials in a secure place until they are needed for the comparison and identification phases of the experiment.

3. On the day of the forgery laboratory session, you will receive one questioned exemplar from your instructor. You will be asked to identify the author of the questioned exemplar by comparing the questioned writing on the questioned exemplar with the writing on each set of known exemplars.

Report

1. Report your findings in the space below. Identify the author of your questioned document by the code number on the known set of exemplars.

2. Justify your conclusions.

3. List matching features of the questioned and known handwritings.

4. Take several black-and-white photographs of the similar characteristics you used to identify the author of the questioned exemplar.

Experiment 25

Soil Examination

Purpose

This chapter will introduce some of the techniques used in the examination and comparison of soil specimens. The student will learn the concepts, rationales, and procedures necessary to collect, examine, and compare forensic soil evidence. Soil is a ubiquitous material that often serves as physical evidence in forensic casework. Soil from the sole of a shoe or vehicle can associate a suspect with a crime scene. Questioned soil specimens can reveal the environment of a crime and help reconstruct the details.

This experiment requires preliminary preparation. Two to three weeks before the experiment will be performed, each student should bring to class a 16-oz soil specimen obtained from an area around his or her home. These specimens will be used to prepare questioned and known samples.

Equipment and Supplies

1. A set of sieves in 20, 40, 60, 80, 100, 150, and 200 mesh sizes and a trap
2. Triple beam balance
3. Six test tubes (6-in.) and six 100-mL beakers
4. Litmus paper
5. Distilled water
6. Munsell soil color chart
7. Disposable plastic pipettes
8. Disposable plastic spot plates
9. Wax pencil or marker
10. Test tube rack
11. Questioned and known soil specimens provided by instructor

Procedure

1. Obtain one questioned and four known soil specimens from your instructor.

2. Air dry and weigh each 100-mL beaker. Record the weight of each beaker on the soil data tabulation sheet below (Table 25.1). Label one beaker Q1 (Q = questioned) and the remainder K1 (K = known) through K4.

3. Place each specimen into its corresponding beaker, e.g., the questioned specimen should be placed into the Q1 beaker.

4. Weigh each specimen and record its weight in Table 25.1.

5. Sieve each specimen using the sieves of different meshes, starting with size 20. After sieving, place the sieved fraction (SF) on a piece of weighing paper. Weigh the fraction and record its weight on Table 25.1.

6. Clean the sieve. Repeat the sieving and weighing steps for each specimen and sieve size.

7. Place a small quantity of each questioned soil (use the 150-mesh fraction) into individual wells of the spot plates and mark for identification. Place a similar size fraction of the known specimen into one of the top wells as depicted in Figure 25.1.

8. Figure 25.1 shows how you would compare the colors of questioned and known specimens. Compare the colors of your soil specimens while they are illuminated by sunlight. Note results on Table 25.2.

9. More precise comparison can be achieved by using a Munsell® soil color chart. To order a chart, call 1-800-622-2384.

10. Place a small quantity of each soil specimen into a labeled test tube. Add 3 to 4 mL of neutral, deionized, distilled water into each test tube and shake well. Place each tube in the rack and allow the soil specimens to settle. With a disposable plastic pipette, draw out a small quantity of water from each test tube and apply it to the litmus test paper. Determine the pH of each specimen and record the results in the Report section below.

TABLE 25.1
Soil Data Weight Sheet

Specimen	Beaker Wt.	Soil Wt.	Total Wt.	Wt. SF 20	Wt. SF 40	Wt. SF 60	Wt. SF 80	Wt. SF 100	Wt. SF 150	Wt. SF 200
Q1										
K1										
K2										
K3										
K4										

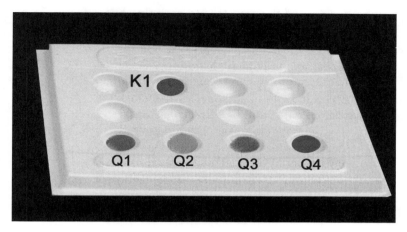

FIGURE 25.1
The preparation of questioned and known soil samples for color comparison.

TABLE 25.2
Color Comparison Table

Specimen	Soil Color (Same or Different)
Q1	
K1	
K2	
K3	
K4	

169

Report

1. Prepare a chart that contains all the data you collected for each soil specimen. Based on the chart, determine whether any of the questioned samples has a common origin with the known specimen.

2. Justify your conclusions.

3. List the similar and dissimilar features of the questioned and known specimens.

4. What is soil?

5. What is the composition of soil?

6. How many minerals are normally contained in an average soil specimen?

7. Could any of the questioned samples be eliminated from the vegetation present in the 20-mesh fraction?

8. Were you able to eliminate any questioned specimens by comparing their soil fractions?

9. Were you able to eliminate any questioned soil specimens by color comparison?

10. What were the pH values of all your specimens? Were any questioned soil specimens eliminated after pH comparison?

Bibliography

Abbott, J.R., *Footwear Evidence*, Charles C Thomas, Springfield, IL, 1964.

Adoryan, A.S. and Kolenosky, G.B., *A Manual for the Identification of Hairs of Selected Ontario Mammals,* Research Report 90, Ontario Department of Lands and Forests, Toronto, 1969.

Alakija, P., Dowling, G.P., and Gunn, B., Stellate clothing defects with different firearms, projectiles, ranges and fabrics, *J. Forens. Sci.,* 43, 1148, 1998.

American Association of Textile Chemists and Colorists, Research Triangle Park, NC, *Technical Manual*, Vol. 53, 1977.

American Society of Crime Laboratory Directors, Laboratory Accreditation Board, *ASCLD-LAB Accreditation Manual*, Largo, FL, 1997.

Antoci, P.R. and Petraco, N., A technique for comparing soil colors in the forensic laboratory, *J. Forens. Sci.,* 38, 437, 1993.

Appleyard, H.M., *Guide to the Identification of Animal Fibres*, 2nd ed., WIRA, Leeds, U.K., 1978.

Ashbaugh, D.R., *Quantitative-Qualitative Friction Ridge Analysis: An Introduction to Basic and Advanced Ridgeology*, CRC Press, Boca Raton, FL, 1999.

Baker, J., *Law of Disputed and Forged Documents*, Michie Co., Charlottesville, VA, 1955.

Banner, H. and Conan, B.J., *The Identification of Mammalian Hair*, Iukata Press, Melbourne, Australia, 1974.

Bevel, T. and Gardner, R., *Bloodstain Pattern Analysis: Introduction to Crime Scene Reconstruction*, 2nd ed., CRC Press, Boca Raton, FL, 2002.

Bisbing, R.E., The forensic identification and association of human hair, in *Forensic Science Handbook,* Saferstein, R., Ed., Prentice-Hall, Englewood Cliffs, NJ, 1982.

Bloss, F.D., *Introduction to the Methods of Optical Crystallography,* Saunders, New York, 1961.

Bodziak, W., *Footwear Impression Evidence,* 2nd ed., CRC Press, Boca Raton, FL, 2002.

Brown, F.M., The microscopy of mammalian hair for anthropologists, *Proc. Amer. Phil. Soc.,* 85, 250, 1942.

Burke, T.W. and Rowe, W.F., Bullet ricochet: a comprehensive review, *J. Forens. Sci.,* 37, 1254, 1992.

Brunelle, R. and Reed, R., *Forensic Examination of Ink and Paper*, Charles C Thomas, Springfield, IL, 1984.

Cassidy, M.J., Footwear Identification, Canadian Government Publishing Center, Ottawa, 1980.

Catling, D.M. and Grayson, J.E., *Identification of Vegetable Fibres*, Chapman & Hall, London, 1982.

Conway, J.V.P., *Evidential Documents*, Charles C Thomas, Springfield, IL, 1959.

Cowger, J.F., *Friction Ridge Skin: Comparison and Identification of Fingerprints*, CRC Press, Boca Raton FL, 1993.

Coyote W.A., Ed., *Papermaking Fibers: A Photomicrographic Atlas,* Syracuse University Press, Syracuse, NY, 1980.

Crown, D., *The Forensic Examination of Paint and Pigments*, Charles C Thomas, Springfield, IL, 1968.

Davis, J.E., *Introduction to Tool Marks, Firearms and the Striagraph*, Charles C Thomas, Springfield, IL, 1958.

DeForest, P., Gaensslen, R., and Lee, H., *Forensic Science: An Introduction to Criminalistics.* McGraw Hill, New York, 1983.

Dick, R.M., The identification of handwriting, a brief discussion, Florida Division of the International Association for Identification Semiannual Conference, Sanford, FL, May 26, 1978.

Du Pasquier, E. et al., Evaluation and comparison of casting materials in forensic sciences: application to tool marks and foot/shoe impressions, *Forens. Sci. Int.,* 82, 33, 1996.

Eckert, W., Ed., *Introduction to Forensic Science,* CRC Press, Boca Raton, FL, 1997.

Ellen, D., *The Scientific Examination of Documents: Methods and Techniques*, John Wiley & Sons, New York, 1989.

Federal Bureau of Investigation, The Science of Fingerprints: Classification and Uses, U.S. Government Printing Office, Washington, D.C., 1998.

Fisher, B., *Techniques of Crime Scene Investigation,* 6th ed., CRC Press, Boca Raton, FL, 2000.

Frei-Sulzer, M., Coloured fibres in criminal investigations with special reference to natural fibres, in *Methods of Forensic Science*, Vol. IV, Curry, A.S., Ed., Interscience, New York, 1965, p. 141.

Fulton, C.C., *Modern Microcrystal Tests for Drugs,* John Wiley & Sons, New York, 1969.

Geradts, Z., Keijzer, J., and Keereweer, I., A new approach to automatic comparison of striation marks, *J. Forens. Sci.,* 39, 974, 1994.

Given, B.W., Nehrich, R.B., and Shields, J.C., *Tire Track and Tread Marks*, Gulf, Houston, TX, 1977.

Glaister, J., *A Study of Hairs and Wools Belonging to the Mammalian Group of Animals, Including a Special Study of Human Hair, Considered from Medico-Legal Aspects*, Misr Press, Cairo, 1931.

Glattstein, B. et al., Improved method for shooting distance estimation. Part 1: bullet holes in clothing items, *J. Forens. Sci.,* 45, 801, 2000.

Graves, W.J., Mineralogical soil classification technique for the forensic scientist, *J. Forens. Sci.,* 24, 331, 1979.

Gross, H., *Criminal Investigation,* adapted from Adams, J.C., *System Der Kriminalistik*, Sweet & Maxwell, London, 1924, p. 131.

Hallimond, A.F., *The Polarizing Microscope,* 3rd ed., Vickers Instruments, York, U.K., 1970.

Hamby, J.E., Firearms reference collections: their size, composition and use, *J. Forens. Sci.,* 42, 461, 1997.

Hamm, E.D, Individuality of class characteristics in Converse All-Star footwear, *J. Forens. Ident.,* 39, 277, 1989.

Hamm, E.D., Track identification: a historical overview, *J. Forens. Ident.,* 39, 333, 1989.

Haring, J.V., *The Hand of Hauptmann*, Hamer Publishing, Plainfield, NJ, 1937.

Harrison, W., *Suspect Documents*, Eastern Press, London, 1958.

Hartshorne, N.H. and Stuart, A., *Crystals and the Polarising Microscope,* 4th ed., Edward Arnold Ltd., London, 1970.

Hatcher, J.S., Jury, F.J., and Weller, J., *Firearms Investigation Identification and Evidence*, Stackpole Books, Harrisburg, PA, 1977.

Hausman, L.H., Structural characteristics of the hair of mammals, *Am. Nat.,* 54, 496, 1920.

Heaney, K.D. and Rowe, W.F., The application of linear regression to range-of-fire estimates based on the spread of shotgun pellet patterns, *J. Forens. Sci.,* 28, 433, 1983.

Hicks, J.W., Microscopy of Hair, U.S. Government Printing Office, Washington, D.C., 1977.

Hilton, O., *Scientific Examination of Questioned Documents*, Revised Edition, CRC Press, Boca Raton, FL, 1993.

Hilton, O., *Detecting and Deciphering Erased Pencil Writing*, Charles C Thomas, Springfield, IL, 1991.

Hogg, I.A., *Encyclopedia of Infantry Weapons of World War II*, Thomas Y. Crowell, New York, 1977.

Hogg, I.A., and Adam, R., *Jane's Gun Recognition Guide*, HarperCollins, Glasgow, 1996.

Inman, K. and N. Rudin, *Principles and Practice of Criminalistics: The Profession of Forensic Science*, CRC Press, Boca Raton, FL, 2001.

James, S.H. and Eckert, W., *Interpretation of Bloodstain Evidence at Crime Scenes,* 2nd ed., CRC Press, Boca Raton, FL, 1999.

James, S.H. and Nordby, J., Eds., *Forensic Science: An Introduction to Scientific and Investigative Techniques*, CRC Press, Boca Raton, FL, 2003.

James, S.H., Ed., *Scientific and Legal Applications of Bloodstain Pattern Interpretation*, CRC Press, Boca Raton, FL, 1998.

Kam, M., Fielding, G., and Conn, R., Writer identification by professional document examiners, *J. Forens. Sci.*, 42, 778, 1997.

Kam, M. et al., Signature authentication by forensic document examiners, *J. Forens. Sci.*, 46, 884, 2001.

Kirk, P.L., *Density and Refractive Index*, Charles C Thomas, Springfield, IL, 1951.

Kirk, P.L., *Crime Investigation*, 2nd ed., John Wiley & Sons, New York, 1974.

Kish, P.E. and MacDonell, H.L., Absence of Evidence is not Evidence of Absence, *J. Forens. Ident.*, 46, 160, 1996.

Laber, T.L., Diameter of a bloodstain as a function of origin, distance fallen and volume of drop, *IABPA News*, 2, 12, 1985.

Laber, T.L. and Epstein, B.P., *Bloodstain Pattern Analysis*, Callen Publishing, Minneapolis, MN, 1983.

Lee, H. et.al., *Crime Scene Investigation.* Central Police University Press, Taoyuan, Taiwan, 1994.

Lee, H. and Harris, H., *Physical Evidence in Forensic Science*, Lawyers & Judges Publishing, Tucson, AZ, 2000.

Lee, H. and Gaensslen, R., *Advances in Fingerprint Technology,* 2nd ed., CRC Press, Boca Raton, FL, 2001.

Lee, H., Palmbach, T., and Miller, M., *Henry Lee's Crime Scene Handbook.* Academic Press, London, 2002.

Lesko, J. et al., *New York Police Department Crime Scene Technician's Manual*, New York City Police Department, 1977.

Locard, E., Analysis of dust traces, Part 1, *Am. J. Police Sci.,* 1, 276, 1930.

Locard, E., Analysis of dust traces, Part 2, *Am. J. Police Sci.,* 1, 405, 1930.

Locard, E., Analysis of dust traces, Part 3, *Am. J. Police Sci.,* 1, 496, 1930.

Longhetti, A. and Roche, G.W., Microscopic identification of man-made fibers from the criminalistics point of view, *J. Forens. Sci.*, 3, 303, 1958.

Maehly, A. and Stromberg, L., *Chemical Criminalistics*, Springer-Verlag, Heidelberg, 1981.

Mathews, J.H., *Firearms Identification*, Vols, 1–3, Charles C Thomas, Springfield, IL, 1962.

McDonald, J., *The Police Photographer's Guide*, Photo Text Books, Arlington Heights, IL, 1992.

MacDonell, H.L., *Interpretation of Bloodstains: Physical Considerations,* Wecht, C., Ed., Appleton, New York, 1971, p. 91.

MacDonell, H.L., *Bloodstain Patterns, Revised*, Laboratory of Forensic Science, Corning, NY, 1997.

MacDonell, H.L. and Bialousz, L., Flight Characteristics and Stain Patterns of Human Blood, U.S. Department of Justice, Washington, D.C., 1971.

MacDonell, H.L. and Bialousz, L. *Laboratory Manual on the Geometric Interpretation of Human Bloodstain Evidence*, Laboratory of Forensic Science, Corning, NY, 1973.

MacDonell, H.L. and Brooks, B., *Detection and Significance of Blood in Firearms*, Wecht, C., Ed., Appleton, New York, 1977.

Man-Made Fiber Producers Association, Washington, D.C., *Man-Made Fibers Fact Book*, 1978.

McCrone, W.C., McCrone, L.B., and Delly, J.G., *Polarized Light Microscopy,* Ann Arbor Science, Ann Arbor, MI, 1978.

McCrone, W.C. and Delly, J.G., *The Particle Atlas*, 2nd ed., Ann Arbor Science, Ann Arbor, MI, 1973.

Meng, H. and Caddy, B., Gunshot residue analysis: a review, *J. Forens. Sci.,* 42, 553, 1997.

Millard, J.T., *A Handbook on the Primary Identification of Revolvers and Semiautomatic Pistols*, Charles C Thomas, Springfield, IL, 1974.

Miller, E.T., Forensic glass comparisons, in *Forensic Science Handbook*, Saferstein, R., Ed., Prentice-Hall, Englewood Cliffs, NJ, 1982, p. 154.

Moncrief, R.W., *Man-Made Fibers*, 6th ed., Newnes-Butterworth, London, 1975.

Moore, T.D. et al., *Identification of the Dorsal Guard Hairs of Some Mammals of Wyoming*, Bulletin No. 14, Wyoming Game and Fish Department, Cheyenne, 1974.

Muehlberger, R.J. et al., A statistical examination of selected handwriting characteristics, *J. Forens. Sci.*, 22, 206, 1977.

Murray, R.C. and Tedrow, J.C.F., *Forensic Geology,* Rutgers University Press, New Brunswick, NJ, 1975.

National Police Agency (Tokyo), An electrostatic method for lifting footprints, *Intl. Criminal Police Rev.*, 272, 287, 1973.

Ogle, R., *Crime Scene Investigation and Physical Evidence Manual,* Vallejo, CA, 1995.

Ojena, S.M. and De Forest, P., Precise refractive index determinations by the immersion method, using phase contrast microscopy and the Mettler Hotstage, *J. Forens. Sci. Soc.*, 12, 315, 1972.

Paine, N., Use of cyanoacrylate fuming and related enhancement techniques to develop shoe impressions on various surfaces, *J. Forens. Ident.*, 48, 585, 1998.

Palenik, S., Microscopy and microchemistry of physical evidence, in *Forensic Science Handbook*, Saferstein, R., Ed., Prentice-Hall, Englewood Cliffs, NJ, 1988, chap. 4.

Palenik, S.J., Microscopical examination of fibers, in *Forensic Examination of Fibers*, Robertson, J. and Grieve, M., Eds., Taylor & Francis, Philadelphia, 1999, chap. 7.

Parham, R.A. and Gray, R.L., *The Practical Identification of Wood Pulp Fibers*, Tappi Press, Atlanta, GA, 1982.

Petraco, N., A modified technique for the cross-sectioning of hairs and fibers, *J. Police Sci. Admin.*, 9, 448, 1981.

Petraco, N. and Kubic, T., *Atlas of Microscopy for Criminalists, Chemists and Conservators*, CRC Press, Boca Raton, FL, in press.

Petraco, N., Resua, R., and Harris, H.H., A rapid method for the preparation of transparent footwear test prints, *J. Forens. Sci.*, 27, 935, 1982.

Petraco, N., Trace evidence — the invisible witness, *J. Forens. Sci.*, 31, 321, 1986.

Petraco, N., The replication of hair cuticle scale catterns in Meltmount, *Microscope*, 34, 341, 1986.

Petraco, N., A guide to the rapid screening, identification, and comparison of synthetic fibers in dust samples, *J. Forens. Sci.*, 32, 768, 1987.

Petraco, N., A microscopical method to aid in the identification of animal hair, *Microscope*, 35, 83, 1987.

Petraco, N. and DeForest, P.R., A guide to the analysis of forensic dust specimens, in *Forensic Science Handbook*, Saferstein, R., Ed., Prentice-Hall, Englewood Cliffs, NJ, 1993, chap. 2.

Pex, J.O. and Vaughn, C.H., Observations of high velocity blood spatter on adjacent objects, *J. Forens. Sci.*, 32, 1587, 1987.

Pizzola, P.A., Roth, S., and DeForest, P.R., Blood droplet dynamics I, *J. Forens. Sci.*, 31, 36, 1986.

Pizzola, P.A., Roth, S., and DeForest, P.R., Blood droplet dynamics II, *J. Forens. Sci.*, 31, 50, 1986.

Redsicker, D., *Practical Methodology of Forensic Photography*, 2nd ed., CRC Press, Boca Raton, FL, 2001.

Risinger, D.M., Denbeaux, M.P., and Saks, M.J., Exorcism of ignorance as a proxy for rational knowledge: the lessons of handwriting identification expertise, *Univ. Penn. Law Rev.*, 137, 731,1989.

Robertson, J. and Grieve, M., Eds., *Forensic Examination of Fibers*, Taylor & Francis, Philadelphia, 1999.

Robertson, J., Ed., *Forensic Examination of Hair*, Taylor & Francis, London, 1999.

Rowe, W.F., Statistics in forensic ballistics, in *The Use of Statistics in Forensic Science*, Aitken, C.G.G. and Stoney, D.A., Eds., Ellis Harwood, New York, 1991.

Rowe, W.F. and Hanson, S.R., Range-of-fire estimates from regression analysis applied to the spread of shotgun pellet patterns: results of a blind study, *Forens. Sci. Int.*, 28, 239, 1985.

Saferstein, R., *Criminalistics: An Introduction to Forensic Science*, 7th ed., Prentice-Hall, Englewood Cliffs, NJ, 2001.

Saferstein, R., Ed., *Forensic Science Handbook*, 2nd ed. Prentice-Hall, Englewood Cliffs, NJ, 2000.

Sansone, S.J., *Police Photography*, Anderson Inc., Cincinnati, 1977.

Sato, H.,Yoshino, M., and Seta, S., Macroscopical and microscopical studies of mammalian hairs with special reference to morphological differences, *Rep. Nat. Res. Inst. Police Sci.*, 33, 1, 1980.

Scott, C.C., *Photographic Evidence*, 2nd ed., West Publishing, St. Paul, MN, 1969.

Shaffer, S.A., Protocol for the examination of hair evidence, *Microscope*, 30, 151, 1982.

Smith, S. and Glaister, J., *Recent Advances in Forensic Medicine*, 2nd ed., Blakiston's Son & Co., Philadelphia, 1939, p. 118.

Söderman, H. and Fontell, E., *Handbok I. Kriminalteknik*, Stockholm, 1930, p. 534.

Stephens, B.G. and Allen, T.B., Back spatter of blood from gunshot wounds: observations and experimental simulation, *J. Forens. Sci.*, 28, 437, 1983.

Stoiber, R.E. and Morse, S.A., *Crystal Identification with the Polarizing Microscope*, Chapman & Hall, New York, 1994.

Streit, C., The hidden message in handwriting, *Law Enforce. Tech.*, 96, Sept. 2001.

Sutton, T.P., *Bloodstain Pattern Analysis in Violent Crimes*, University of Tennessee Press, Memphis, 1993.

Textile Institute, *Identification of Textile Materials*, Manchester, U.K., 1970.

Theeuwen, A.B.E. and Limborgh, J.C.M., Comparison of chemical methods for the visualization and enhancement of footwear impressions in blood, *Forens. Sci. Int.,* 95, 133, 1998.

Thorwald, J., *Crime and Science*, Harcourt, Brace, New York, 1966, p. 280.

TWGMAT, *Forensic Fiber Examination Guidelines*, Fiber Subgroup, Washington, D.C., 1998.

U.S. Department of Commerce, Reference Collection of Synthetic Fibers, National Bureau of Standards, Washington, D.C., January 1984.

White, R.B., Bloodstain patterns of fabrics: effects of drop volume, dropping height and impact angle, *J. Can. Soc. Forens. Sci.,* 19, 3, 1983.

Wildman, A.B., *Microscopy of Animal Textile Fibres*, WIRA, Leeds, U.K., 1954.